THE SEALED MAGICAL BOOK OF MOSES

By William Alexander Oribello

Inner Light/Global Communications

THE SEALED MAGICAL BOOK OF MOSES

I wish to dedicate this work to the true seekers of the path of Light throughout the planet. May they find within these pages the inspiration and guidance to evolve in the glorious work of Higher Magic.

The Great Cosmic Guardians have directed me to eliminate the non-essential elements of magical ritual and get to the heart of one of the powerful branches of the Great Work. No one book can cover all stages of the Holy Art: this book is a channel to aid the student in the mastery of Moses' Magical Spirit Art, which can be the very source of the student's personal attainment in all matters of life.

Should the student wish to pursue even greater mysteries of the Secret Wisdom teachings, and the higher initiations, he or she is invited to write the author for more information concerning the Inner Teachings of Christ. Address such requests to:

FREE SUBSCRIPTION TO OUR WEEKLY NEWSLETTER AVAILABLE AT -
WWW.CONSPIRACYJOURNAL.COM

ISBN-13: 978-0938294689
ISBN-10: 0938294687

Contents

The Sealed Magical Book of Moses

1. THE SECRET OF MOSES

In an ancient age when magic was an everyday occurrence, there was a race of "wise ones" who preserved and taught a higher form of magic that attuned the practitioner with the highest manifestation of universal wisdom. Such a wise one was the great Prophet known as Moses. From the grade of mystic adept to mastery, this great soul rediscovered a sacred magical system that has never been fully or plainly expounded in writing until now.

OTHER MAGICAL BOOKS OF MOSES:

In addition to the five Biblical Books that have been attributed to Moses, there is also the belief that Moses authored five more books which revealed the secret of his magic miracle-working power. Some manuscripts have emerged throughout history, which describe mysterious talismans and practices said to have been used by Moses himself to work his great wonders. However, the manuscripts which have come down to us are difficult to understand in that they are written in symbolic terms. Furthermore, medieval magicians added many of their own ideas to the manuscripts that emerged during that period in Germany. As any thinking person realizes that even the Bible was added to during its various translations, it is not difficult to believe that the magical works were also changed to suit the trend of thinking at different periods of time.

WHAT IS THE SEALED MAGICAL BOOK OF MOSES?:

In this book you are now reading the author reveals anew the simple, yet powerful wisdom that Moses originally learned and taught. This wisdom concerns the original use of the different symbols and magical formulas which have become known as Moses[1] Magical Spirit Art. Mastering this art will give the student power over the forces of nature and create a flow of good fortune, happiness and personal power, when applied correctly.

HOW THIS BOOK CAME TO THE AUTHOR:

There has never been a time in my life when I was not aware of my divine calling. My memory takes me back to infancy, when in my crib, helpless and unable to communicate. There was always that awareness of a higher knowledge, but alas, my present incarnation in physical matter was a block which I had to overcome in search of the wisdom which would bring about my re-awakening to what I was all about and why I was here. Visions and periods of realization were frequent in my early years. I remember one autumn night, I looked up at the stars and suddenly felt an awareness and kinship with all life. What a glorious realization that was!

In addition to the visions and awareness of supernatural beings around me, I also began to meet ordinary humans who became a lasting influence on my life. I say ordinary humans; but the people I refer to were more than just ordinary humans. These blessed souls were members of a secret society that has existed since the beginning of life on this planet. When I use the term, secret society, I do not mean any religious denomination or cult. What I refer to is that in all ages there have been groups of people in all nations who have preserved the true Secret Wisdom of God that governs the universal magical laws of mind and nature.

One such person was a medical doctor from India. He became friends with my family and came to dinner one evening. As soon as we were alone in the living room for a few moments, he began to communicate with me in such a manner so as to let me know that he was aware of the inner experiences I was having. He said that I was an advanced soul returned to earth for a mission and that I would rediscover and teach lost wisdom to humankind. He also gave me instructions to follow which I cannot reveal here, and assured me that other visitations would follow throughout my life.

The next visitor was from Jamaica. This man gave me a document which decoded the Bible. I had begun reading the Holy Bible and realized that there was great wisdom hidden in a carefully designed code of stories and symbols. This man gave me the key that unlocked the door of the Biblical Mysteries.

Now, concerning the secret of Moses; at the age of eleven I met a certain lady who gave me a copy of a book called "the 6th, and 7th books of Moses". She told me that when I read this it would awaken a memory locked within my inner mind. This memory was of the different times when I lived on earth before and learned the Secret wisdom of the Ages. However, she admonished me not to take the book literally, for it was not the complete magical book of Moses. She informed me that there was a book which has not been published for thousands of years, and even then was just exposed to a few wise adepts. She said that if I studied the book she gave me for many years, that one day my inner sight would be opened and my memory would go back to the misty past and the complete formula would be revealed again to me so that I could now share it with those who were hungry and thirsty for the true knowledge. That day has come.

One of the greatest visions I wish to share is that of the appearance of the Three Wisemen. Materialization is more accurate of a word than vision. It was at the age of seventeen. I was awakened in the middle of the night by three men dressed in the garb of the Magi, as illustrated in the pictures of their visit to the Christ child. These beings were surrounded by a radiant light. They spoke several comforting words concerning the current events of my life and the future.

Then the Magi showed me a large, old looking "book. It resembled an aged family Bible. They opened the book and on its pages was written a vast knowledge concerning all the mysteries of life that can be known by a human. It was as though someone wrote with a quill pen on the pages. Throughout the night I read the book with superhuman speed, and then the illustrious masters left me with a message: they said that the Word was now in my heart, and that I would remember the wisdom only when it was required to help others. I was also informed that at a later time I would write several books which would reveal the Ageless Wisdom once again in a manner that could -be easily understood by all. That time is now. The wisdom of the true Word can be found in the various books I have written, and the ones that are to come.

Since that time I have spoken to countless thousands of people and have communicated to other great beings including Moses. In this manner I am now able to bring you this tome of the Secret Wisdom regarding the original simple magical formula of Moses.

WHO WAS MOSES?:

According to the Biblical account of Moses' life we learn that he was born during a turbulent period in the history of the Hebrew Nation. The King of Egypt feared the growing population of Hebrews and ordered that all male children be killed, and the females allowed to live. When Moses was born his mother kept him for three months, and when she could no longer hide him she prepared an ark of bulrushes, laid the child in it and set it afloat on the river committing him into the hands of God. Pharaoh's daughter discovered the child in the ark floating on the Nile, and the princess kept and raised Moses as her own son.

As Moses grew, he obtained the knowledge of his true nation and set about trying to free his people from Egyptian oppression. He went so far as to murder an Egyptian taskmaster who was beating a Hebrew. Because of this he became the target of persecution from Pharaoh and had to leave Egypt for his own safety.

Moses went to the land of Midian where he married the daughter of Jethro, the Priest of Midian. After many years of living in this family and land something happened that changed Moses' life for all time: one day, as he kept the flock of his father-in-law he saw a vision of a mysterious fire which turned in a bush, yet did not destroy the bush. Out of this fire he heard the voice of God which gave him a message and power to return to Egypt and liberate his people from bondage. Thus is a portion of the literal account within scripture. But, let us examine this story further as to its inner meaning.

All characters and stories in the scriptures are there for a reason; they represent certain processes of inner development which all people experience in the evolution of life and consciousness. I am not saying that the Biblical characters did not exist as real people. I believe that they did. However, as an initiate of the Ageless Wisdom I know that the various accounts of these people are symbolic of inner keys of understanding and realization which could only be communicated in this manner.

The inner significance of the name Moses means drawing (extracting) from the water. The land of Egypt is known as both the place of wisdom and the land of darkness among the inner circle of initiates. Moses' nation was in a state of suffering in Egypt when he was born. This reveals that when we have reached a state of passive being, or darkness, then are we ready to look within that we may extract the true inner power (draw out) to manifest in our daily life. Water represents spiritual thought. Moses[1] mother prepared an ark of bulrushes and set the child adrift on the Nile River. When we have become inactive or negative in a passive sense (as exemplified in the land of darkness-Egypt) we are guided into spiritual thoughts (the river). But to balance ourselves so we are not overwhelmed at the greatness of the path we must pace our work and stay within the domains of both worlds (the ark).

To further illustrate the last statement, let us say that the ark represented something made from the earth. Earth is symbolic of matter, or physical activity, while water is symbolic of thought or spiritual thought. If the child was placed into the water by itself he would have drowned. Therefore the ark of bulrushes was the means by which the child could safely float on the river. Therefore, the inner message of this part of the story is that we should keep ourselves in balance and not try to accomplish too much too quickly in the realm of spiritual thought, but remember that we are still in a body of matter (the ark) and harmonize the two realms that we may 'arrive safely to our goal of illumination. Pharaoh's daughter is symbolic of the intuition of the subconscious mind. According to the account she extracted the child from the water and protected it. This is symbolic of the early stages of mystical development when we allow our intuition to guide us into the victory of bringing forth that hidden man, or the hidden child which has been brought about by spiritual thought activities.

Moses grew and attempted to liberate his people before the time was right. He killed the Egyptian who oppressed his fellow Hebrew. This is symbolic of the fact that we may become zealous without wisdom when we first begin to make progress on the path, and ignore the mental process of constructive reasoning, thinking it to be too mundane. We silence the voice of discipline manifesting in the process of reason (kill the Egyptian), and hide it in the illusions of matter (we bury the Egyptian in the sand). This leads us to have to learn our lessons the hard way: Moses was driven from Egypt into the wilderness. This is symbolic of what happens when we feel we can advance spiritually without the needed discipline. We go into what has been termed the dry spell or period of seeming inactivity until we are ready to enter into the kingdom within the right way. Moses means to draw out-to bring forth the power if the inner self into everyday reality.

Moses went to the land of Midian and married Jethro's daughter. He also kept the flocks of his father-in-law Jethro for forty years. This is symbolic of when we go within to undergo self imposed discipline that we cultivate our thoughts (flocks) in the development of correct reasoning (the land of Midian). Forty years is symbolic of mastering the four lower bodies: the physical, vital (etheric double), astral and mental. It also means that we receive a well rounded spiritual education to complete our progress. Are there not four sides to a house?

When we train our thoughts to go to the quiet place (the backside of the desert) we reach the region of the I AM or higher mind. It is then that we behold the fire of illumination which burns.

Let us examine the mystery of the "burning bush more closely. This is symbolic of the Cosmic Fire resident within each human, but dormant in most. The bush is symbolic of the inner, or Sympathetic Nervous System which is part of the psychic centers in the physical body. The fire has been termed Kundalini by Eastern teachers of the occult wisdom. This fire resides at the base of the spine (the fire is a psycho-physiological energy). As we channel our energy, thoughts and attention into avenues of higher spiritual thought this fire rises up awakening the spinal psychic centers until it reaches the brain and opens the inner eye, causing self-realization and cosmic consciousness. The fire has also been called the serpent. When it is dormant at the base of the spine it is termed the 'serpent of sin' or he who eats dust. But when it has risen to the brain it is termed 'the upraised serpent of wisdom' This is why Jesus said, "as Moses lifted up the serpent in the wilderness, even so must the Son of man be lifted up". St. John 3:14. When this awakening is accomplished the ordinary person (Son of man) is lifted up and becomes a great person (Son of God). I should also add that in normal thinking there is a certain vibration set in motion which uses up nerve tissue (it consumes the bush). But, when we allow our higher mind to think the fire saturates our whole being and we are aflame with the Fire of the Holy Spirit which does not use up or weaken us in any way (the fire does not consume the bush).

When Moses drew closer to the burning bush he was instructed to remove the shoes from his feet because he was standing on holy ground. Even so, when we approach the higher wisdom we must remove all negative thinking which limits our chances of a more permanent association with the Cosmic Mind. We approach the higher awareness in a state of mental silence-we stand upon the holy ground of the Kingdom of God within, and hear the thunderous voice of the Almighty speaking through a higher portion of our own thinking and identifying himself as "I AM THAT I AM".

Our consideration of Moses in an esoteric sense-has revealed- what we should strive for in our quest for mastery in the holy magical arts. To master and develop ourselves is the master key which unlocks the door to the revelation of life's mysteries. Another noteworthy reflection is that there are five letters in the name Moses. This reminds us of the five points of the pyramid; the four side at the base, and the apex. The pyramid is a grand example of the building ability of man. Even so, Moses represents the possibilities of every person in their quest for self-mastery.

And now, our next consideration will be the origin of Moses' magical art, and how we can achieve the same results. All that I have said up until now is to prepare you to enter a practical path to achieve the great work in your life.

THE ORIGIN OF MOSES' MAGICAL ART:

From the misty past come legends of a secret Divine Wisdom which gave its students the keys to Heaven. It is said that this wisdom was first taught to select angels by none other than the Almighty God. Later when the race of spirits, now called humankind, plunged into dense matter (expelled from Eden), the angels taught this wisdom to mankind as a means for the human race to find its way back to the perfection of God. Select individuals became masters and custodians of this secret wisdom and passed it down from teacher to pupil from generation to generation. This powerful teaching was imparted by a graded system termed degrees of initiation, by which the students received instructions step by step until they saturated his or her total consciousness.

Ancient tradition reveals that this wisdom reached a golden age of development in the legendary Atlantis. The mystical priests of Atlantis guided the population into great advancement of inner, as well as scientific development. Many of our modern day scientific developments would be dwarfed by the technology of Atlantis. However, the greed and corruption of the bulk of the priestcraft of that glorious land caused a decline which led to the destruction of the Atlantean Utopia.

The true believers fled to several distant lands and, preserving the sacred wisdom, established advanced institutions of learning.

One of the great institutions, or mystery- schools, was established in ancient Egypt. A mysterious person called Thoth was believed to be the Grand Master of the Universal Wisdom. Thoth was also known as Hermes Trismegistus, or 'Thrice Great Hermes'. It was written that Thoth blessed humankind by revealing the secrets of magical philosophy, medicine, chemistry, music, art and other sciences. Thoth received his knowledge from God and wrote countless books of wisdom.

It is believed that Thoth was an immortal, and was later known as Enoch, of whom the Bible says that he walked 'with God and was translated into the higher realms so that his physical body did not taste of death. To the Greek philosophers he was known as the god Mercury. The mystery schools of all ages regard him as the hidden master of the Universal Divine Wisdom. This is why true mystical knowledge is sometimes referred to as Hermetic.

THE BOOK OF THOTH:

It is known among true initiates of God's Wisdom that there exists a great book which reveals the mysteries of life. It is written, concerning some of the master teachers, that they read a great book of wisdom. It is called the Book 'T' (Book of Thoth). At times it is called the Book 'M' (Book of Mercury). The true book of Thoth is not some physical book, but the Book of Life which can only he read by one who has been inspired by the Holy Spirit and with the guidance of the Ascended Masters of the Wisdom. This was my experience when the three illustrious visitors appeared and opened the Great Book to me. However, there did exist a physical book which prepared the student to read the higher book of the secret wisdom. It is believed that this book was written by Thoth, and that Moses was one of the humans of that day who read and mastered that book. Later in this work I will reveal the symbols and instructions of the Book of Thoth, which opens the eyes of the student so that he may prepare to read the greater book. This' was closely "guarded in past ages, except for a select few. But in this hour it can now be taught more openly. This process will open and awaken dormant centers within the student when applied according to the instructions I will give. This awakening gives the student power over the spirits, and the elements. It also gives the inner wisdom needed to compel the forces embodied in the sacred magical talismans to assist us in our work for God, and the good of all concerned.

As time passed, the secret wisdom was gathered into one body of instruction and termed "the Kabala". This name was used by the Hebrew mystics throughout the ages. The Prophets, such as Samuel and Elijah established wisdom schools and called them the School of the Prophets. The Persian mystic established the Order of the Holy Magi. The Egyptian mystics gave their instructions in the hidden chambers of the Great Pyramid, and the list goes on of the fact of how the mystics of all nations established mystery schools in every century.

TRUE INITIATES AND FALSE MAGICIANS:

To possess the hidden wisdom gives one certain powers over the laws of nature, to communicate with nature's finer forces in such a manner so as to display what may be called a miracle by the uninitiated. But, not all initiates used their power for the good of all concerned.

The magician was given the knowledge of the virtues of certain herbs and roots, the powers within certain symbols and words when inscribed on talismans; and the ability to communicate with angelic beings, spirits of the departed, and the beings of the elements. Most of them wore a distinct garment which identified them and owned a staff or wand inscribed with symbols of power. An example of the magical wand is found in the story of Moses: God gave him the ability to cast down his staff so that the staff become a wriggling serpent. When he performed this wonder in the presence of the King of Egypt, the king's magicians were able to duplicate this wonder-with one exception-Moses' serpent swallowed up their serpents. Moses was a true initiate of God's wisdom, but those who opposed him were among the false magicians who perverted the sacred science to satisfy their own selfish ends. This perversion is often called Black Magic or Sorcery, and we find its roots in the Atlantean Epoch which led to the destruction of the continent.

Later, in Egypt, evil magicians worked to hinder the true schools in that land. At one point of Egyptian History, the false magicians were actually the ruling force behind the throne. They blocked the path of wisdom and hid the keys of knowledge so that the way of attainment would be hard to find even by the sincere seeker. This they did to control the masses with dogmatic religious beliefs, fear and superstition which still affects humankind today. This same perversion prevailed in Israel; after Moses, the great prophet passed from life, certain scribes perverted the Law, making it a burden rather than salvation. Jesus exposed this universal crime when he denounced the priestcraft of his time. Even after the birth of Christianity, false prophets perverted the true message of the Christ so that now, two thousand years later, it has become a theater of conflict between disagreeing sects and denominations.

The sacred science of Thoth which was the fountainhead of Moses' great power, was misused by the evil ones who left the true path of Light Many magicians of the middle ages polluted the Magical Art of Moses by introducing rituals of black magic whereby the sacred hieroglyphics and Divine Names were defiled through the invocation of demoniacal spirits to aid the false worker in achieving his selfish ends. This led to making pacts with the devil, diabolical rites involving corpses and horrible rituals of human sacrifice. Furthermore, they changed the meanings of the sacred symbols so that it would be difficult to understand the Divine Formula of Power. Many such magicians became obsessed with the idea of literally turning lead into gold by means of their power. Some lost their minds, and their lives in this quest.' While the Universal Mind has revealed that it is able to Impart this knowledge of gold making to the blameless disciple when needed, it reminds us that the greatest ability is to transmute the lead of a mundane life into the gold of a spiritually vibrant life. Although the forces of darkness have done a great deal to pervert the path of wisdom, there has always been the secret societies of the Light who have worked hard to make the way of attainment open to the sincere seeker of wisdom and knowledge that lead Godward.

THE MAGIC STAR:

Twenty centuries ago, three members of the Order of the Holy Magi followed a star in search of a newborn child. They knew that this child represented the possibilities of all men; all men possess the inner keys to become a self-realized Son of God. All of us have the potential to graduate from hu-man to God-man, that we may manifest the nature of the celestial Adam into our human form, and thus accomplish the true alchemical transmutation of lead into gold. Jesus the Christ was an advanced soul who completed the journey from humanity to divinity, then returned to give us the lost keys and perfect the existing system of the true and higher magic of the soul.

In the centuries following his appearance on earth, there has always been the hidden order of brothers and sisters of the Light who preserve the sacred sciences, even during times of spiritual ignorance and global tribulation. The magical star "still shines brightly to guide us to the revelation of the Christ within, if we but turn our gaze to the higher concepts of life. Also, the magic star has been embodied with its concepts in the symbol of the Pentagram, of which I will teach more as we progress in this present work.

THE NEW AGE:

This is the hour in which these great mysteries shall be revealed in all their simplicity and glory as was intended by God since the beginning. Dear friend, my eyes have beheld the glory of the Lord and his divine messengers, and I will not withhold the truth that must now be given. Therefore, drink deeply of the well of wisdom and be blessed. But, beware-you must use this knowledge to help and not hinder, for they who misuse this power shall come to a horrible end.

2. THE BOOK OF THOTH REVEALED

Mystic tradition reveals that Moses was initiated into the secret wisdom of the Egyptian mystery schools, and that wisdom originated from the teachings of Thoth, or Hermes, as discussed in the last chapter. It is believed that Moses read the physical Book of Thoth which prepares the human mind to perceive the greater knowledge contained in God's Book of Life which can never be written by human hands.

MOSES' SECRET NAME:

The initiates "of the mystery schools (also called wisdom schools) received another name that characterized their degree of progress. Examples of this are found in the Holy Bible: when any person advanced spiritually they would receive a visitation from an angel, see a vision or hear a voice informing them that they have been given a new name symbolic of their advanced progress. Abram's name was changed to Abraham (see Genesis 17:5); Jacob's name was changed to Israel (Genesis 32:28); Saul received the name St. Paul (Acts 13:9); Jesus promised that all overcomers would receive a secret stone, and on the stone a new secret name (Revelation 2:17).

Moses was given a secret name of power, and that name could not be revealed until now.

The secret name of Moses is SHEMMAH and means a great shining one-like the Sun. It is the time that this should be revealed, and the person who is active in the work of this book should have the Holy Shemmah Medallion; for to wear the secret name of Moses is to increase our effectiveness in the sacred magical work. I will teach further of The Holy Shemmah Medallion later in this volume.

The first thing we must do is prepare the student's mind to be awakened to the higher mysteries by revealing the Book of Thoth.

The preservation of Thoth's great wisdom was accomplished by inscribing the hieroglyphic symbols into a deck of cards known as Tarot or Taro.

It is written that the Magi first preserved the symbols of Thoth in pictures or illustrations. The Gypsies helped to preserve the Taro from generation to generation. While the Tarot cards are generally used as a medium of psychic readings or divination, There is a great deal of hidden knowledge in their symbolism.

The Tarot contains pictures of the story of humankind, and if used according to a special formula of observation, can unlock the door to our higher awareness. Special attention should be given to the 22 major arcana to do this.

The 22 letters of the Hebrew Alphabet are in harmony with the 22 cards we shall consider, and I must admonish the student that it is extremely important to follow the instructions set forth in this chapter as it will set in motion the inner abilities of achieving power in life.

You may wish to obtain your own deck of Tarot Cards for suggested meditations. However, I have included illustrations of the 22 cards in this chapter for your convenience. If you do purchase a deck, I suggest you obtain the Rider Tarot Deck.

You must be relaxed and alone when meditating according to my instructions. Read the 22 words of power, with their prescribed scripture as recorded in the 119th. Psalm in the Holy Bible.

ALEPH - The Fool Psalm 119: 1-8
Aleph means strength of spirit.

The Fool walks towards the edge of a cliff but seems oblivious to danger. He holds a white flower in his left hand under a white sun, and looks towards the sky. This is symbolic of man who came from God (the Sun), and is part of God (the flower), ever gazing upward in search of the source of his being. One thing worthy of notice is that he looks in the opposite direction of the Sun (man's present nature inclines him away from God until he is regenerated). The Pool is the true self, stepping out into matter. As the spirit begins its long journey into material manifestation, it leaves the high place (notice the white mountains). However, it is followed by a white dog which is symbolic of the inner mind, always trying to get our attention, ever ready to serve us.

BETH - The Magician Psalm 119: 9-16
Beth means house.

The higher self observes the manifestation of his existence: on the table are the four symbolic tools of Magic. The Wand, symbolic of the element of Fire; The Cup, symbolic of the element of Water; The Sword, symbolic of the element of Air; and the Pentacle, symbolic of the element of Earth. In front of the table is a bush of lilies, and roses. This is symbolic of development through all experiences, for Christ said, "I am the lily of the valley" (low place-the valley), "and the rose of sharon"(high place-sharon). The Magician holds a white scroll which he points to the heavens. This is symbolic of holding on to the Light of higher understanding. With the other hand he points to the Earth which means he recognizes the presence of God everywhere, even in physical matter. St. Anthony, upon "being asked what books he read to attain such power, pointed to the heavens and to the earth and said, "these are my books". Above the magician's head is the number eight written horizontally. This reveals the intended harmony between the conscious and subconscious mind. Eight symbolizes the occult axiom. "As above, so below" as it is in heaven so may it be on earth. Remember, Beth means house. Beth-El (Bethel) means the House of God, and you are the Temple or House of God.

GIMEL - The High Priestess Psalm 119: 17-24
Gimel means camel.

In this card we see the symbolic images of Isis, the Virgin Mary, and Mother God. She holds a scroll on which the word Tora (the law) is written. It is partially hidden, symbolic of the secret wisdom which is hidden within the faculties of the inner mind. The High Priestess sits in the temple between two pillars: a black one on her right and a white one on her left. The black pillar displays the letter B for Boaz, and is symbolic of your conscious mind. The white pillar displays the letter J for Jachin and is symbolic of your subconscious mind. The High Priestess in the center tells us that by going within through meditation, we create a condition of harmony between our conscious and subconscious levels of awareness. When we think of the camel we visualize two humps, and this symbolism is contained in the two pillars as conscious and subconscious mind. The cross on her chest reveals that, above all, the way of the heart (love) is the means by which we accomplish this balance and harmony.

DALETH - The Empress Psalm 119: 25-32
Daleth means door.

Again we see the feminine principle in a different way: The Empress (your inner mind) rules over her house, and is symbolic of your subconscious becoming stronger and letting go of negative restrictions. At her right is a heart with the symbol of Venus (love) which again reminds us that the way of the heart is the means to achieve this state of being. She holds the golden scepter of the Divine Kingdom and wears a crown of 12 stars (symbolic of the qualities of the 12 Apostles within you). The Empress wears a string of pearls (as in "Pearls of Wisdom) which is symbolic of adorning ourselves with the beauty of wisdom. To her left is a tree that stands out from the rest; it is in the shape of a pinecone which is an ancient symbol for the Pineal Gland (the physical center for the Third Eye of psychic, vision). This reveals that by training ourselves to become receptive we are blessed with influences from higher levels of life.

HEH - The Emperor Psalm 119: 33-40
Heh means window.

It has been said, "the eyes are the window of the soul". When we have developed inner sight, we also see things differently in the outer world. The Emperor is symbolic of the conscious mind (masculine principle) awakening to an illuminated awareness. He sits on a throne of stone (symbolic of the Rock of Ages, or Truth). There are four Rams' heads carved on the throne which reveals that by determination we uncover the mysteries of the elemental kingdom (the physical realm). The Emperor is one who rules the outer and the inner mind. In his left hand is the golden globe (inner mind). In his right hand is the Ankh, ancient Egyptian

Cross of Life (outer mind). Meditation on the Emperor gives power over our thoughts.

VAU - The Hierophant Psalm 119: 41-48
Vau means nail.

The Hierophant is symbolic of your superconscious mind or High Self. He sits on a throne between two pillars, two persons, and his face between two ribbons of gold on either side of his crown. All of the symbols just mentioned tell us that the superconscious mind is the prime factor of balance-and harmony between the conscious and subconscious mind as we develop on the path. It is also the nail that binds firm all levels of our mental awareness as one. Notice that on the robes of the two persons, one has lilies and the other has roses (review the card of The Magician). At the feet of the Hierophant are two keys which represent faith and love, with the master being hope of a higher life. His heart is crossed with a white strip with three crosses. His white shoes also bear the sign of the cross. This is symbolic of pure emotion and pure action in the physical kingdom. There are also four circles with crosses at his feet which reveal mastery over the kingdom of the four elements. On the crown are three layers with three nails at the top, and he holds a triple cross in his left hand; We are again reminded of the oneness we must achieve in the expression of the three levels of mental awareness. The hierophant raises his right hand in the salutation of the adepts, symbolic of right action and initiation into the Fraternity of Light. His three upraised fingers are part of one hand and signify the trinity, or three in one.

ZAIN - The Lovers Psalm 119: 49-56
Zain means sword.

In this card we notice two humans, male and female, with an angel between and above them. The woman looks towards the angel while the man looks towards the woman. Symbolically, the man represents the conscious mind. The woman represents the subconscious mind, and the angel represents the superconscious mind or high self. The conscious (man) must go within to create harmony with the subconscious (woman), which looks to the superconscious (the angel) to channel inspiration into everyday consciousness. This is the way our mental levels work. The woman is symbolic of the subconscious mind and the sympathetic nervous system; this is illustrated by the tree behind her: the serpent is raised up on the tree which is a sign of regeneration ("as Moses lifted up the serpent...so must the Son of Man he lifted up" St. John 3:14). There are four fruits on the tree, symbolic of the fact that by creating a state of harmony within, we become our own master in the four worlds (the physical world, the astral or emotional world, the mental world and the spiritual world). Behind the man is a tree with twelve fruits, symbolic of developing the Apostolic Qualities within us ("the Tree of Life, which bare twelve manner of fruit"

Revelation 22:2). Since Zain means sword we think of the double edged sword of the word of God ("and out of his mouth went a sharp two-edged sword" Revelation 1:16). When we reach the state of love -between the levels of our mental awareness, we are given the sacred sword "Excalibur" which divides the real from the unreal.

CHETH - The Chariot Psalm 119:57-64
Cheth means fenced field.

A most interesting feature of this card is the Sphinx. On the right side of the driver is the black sphinx (conscious mind). On the left is the white sphinx (the subconscious mind). The sphinx is a symbol of great wisdom, therefore, this card reveals the state of wisdom which the total mind ascends into. The driver is the high self. On his chest is a square amulet that is symbolic of even balance between our physical, emotional, mental and spiritual natures. On his head is the eight-pointed star, symbolic of regeneration. The red symbol that resembles a top on the front of the chariot is an ancient one that represents the balance of sexual energy. Above is the Winged Sun which is another symbol for regeneration. The blue drape with stars above the driver represents mystic knowledge. This card reveals that the field of mental activity should be protected (fenced field) by the high self.

TETH- Strength Psalm 119: 65-72
Teth means serpent.

The serpent is symbolic of wisdom, either regenerated or unregenerated. The animal on the corresponding card is not the serpent but the lion. I will reveal why: in the original story of Adam and Eve, the word translated into serpent is Nachash. The word for the Deliverer or Christ is Nechesk. The same wisdom which is evil in an unregenerated state, becomes the Saviour when regenerated. The scriptures do not refer to the serpent as a symbol for evil alone, but also the symbol of wisdom (be wise as serpents) and sacred power (as Moses lifted up the serpent, so must the Son of Man be lifted up). On the card we find the lion, also called the king of beasts. However, the lion is tamed by the woman in white. This is symbolic of allowing the subconscious mind to tame the beastly nature (carnality) of the conscious mind. The subconscious mind is gentle and pure in its proper state. It also has access to the high self so that it is able to channel wisdom and inspiration to the liberated individual. The woman wears white which is symbolic for purity. Around her waist and head are garlands of red and green, symbolic of inner development and refinement of the appetites. Above her head is the number eight in the same position as above the magician's, symbolic of a new beginning through achieving a state of harmony.

YOD - The Hermit Psalm 119: 73-80
Yod means hand.

A hermit is a person who dwells alone. The symbolism of this card has more than on interpretation. For example, the hermit walks on top of a white mountain, which means our soul is moving upward in search for higher consciousness. When we search for God, we may (and often do) walk the path alone, as a hermit. Another way to interpret this card is to see the hermit as the superconscious level of mental awareness, standing at the summit and holding the light of truth to guide our steps upward. In the lantern we see the sacred symbol of the six pointed star which is formed from two triangles: one pointing up, the other pointing down. This symbol represents the unity we must achieve between the lower and higher expressions of our being. The hermit holds the staff, symbolic of control over the flow of energy within the spinal canal. The word hand (Yod) corresponds to this card because the hands, of the hermit seem to be an outstanding feature of action: the right hand holds the light, the left hand holds the staff.

KAPH - The Wheel of Fortune Psalm 119: 81-88
Kaph means grasping hand.

We will consider this card from its center. The central wheel has four spokes with alchemical symbols: the spoke to the left has the symbol of salt (conscios and physical); to the right is the symbol of sulphur (subconscious and emotional); The upper spoke has the symbol of mercury (super- conscious and mental); The lower has the symbol of Aquarius (spiritual flow or secret process). The Alchemists were said to use the three substances of salt, sulphur and mercury (quick silver). By a secret process they would combine these to produce the "Philosopher's Stone" which would magically transform lead into gold (change the lower nature of man into the higher spiritual state). The four spokes that cross each other like the letter X are symbolic of the physical kingdom. Within the outer circle are four Hebrew Letters that, together, represent the word Tetragrammaton. This word is said to contain ana conceal the unspeakable name of God. Between the Hebrew Letters are the Roman Letters R.O.T.A. They represent a sentence in broken Latin, "Rota Orat'Tora Ator" which means "the Tarot reveals the laws of life". At the top of the wheel sits the Sphinx, symbol of all wisdom in all dimensions, holding the sword which divides the real from the unreal. At the bottom of the wheel a human figure with the head of a Jackal floats in mid air and carries the symbol on its back. To the left of the wheel is the serpent of divine wisdom manifesting within physical matter. The three symbols also represent the three alchemical substances of salt, sulphur and mercury. In the four corners of the card are the symbols of the four elements: the Ox for Earth, the Lion for Fire, the Eagle for Air, and Man for Water. This card seems to be the sum total of the existence and potential of every person. The words "grasping hand" are associated because it reveals that if we grasp the symbolism of the card, we are blessed.

LAMED - Justice Psalm 119: 89-96
Lamed means whip or ox-goad.

The common symbol for Justice is a blindfolded person with a sword in one hand and scales in the other. However, the person m this card is not blindfolded, which means that this represents the higher justice of the Divine Consciousness that sees all. There are two pillars: the one to his left behind the scales is the pillar of the Universal Law. The one behind the sword is the pillar of the Divine Word. Therefore, divine justice is built upon the law and the word of God. The word "whip" is associated to reveal that divine justice may drive us into situations by which we purge ourselves from past mistakes and karmic debts; we must right all wrongs and heal all wounds in this, or another lifetime. When we go through difficult situations and seem to "be getting a subtle message from it all, it is divine justice helping us to clean the books by reaping what we have sown. The crown has three squares, symbolic of balanced harmony between the three levels of mental awareness.

MEM - The Hanged Man Psalm 119: 97-104
Mem means water.

The man is suspended from a tree, which appears to have been cut in half, and one half laid in a horizontal position across the vertical other half. This is the symbol of the "Tau Cross", one of the most ancient, versions of the cross. In some of the ancient mystery schools, the Tau Cross -was made on the forehead of new students with oil or ashes. In some ancient cultures, a Tau Cross was handed to a person who found mercy in a court and was forgiven of a crime. The attitude of the hanged man is positive, for he has a brilliant light around his head which indicates spiritual thinking. His hair has the appearance of flowing water (Mem). Therefore, the outer symbolism of the hanged man reveals a state of willful submission to hanging upside down, but the esoteric meaning reveals more: If we observe the thinking of mass humanity, we quickly realize that anyone who thinks spiritually, with complete sincerity, is thinking in reverse of the accepted way or thinking (upside down). Such a one is often scorned for their beliefs and branded as weird or too old fashioned. However, they are symbolically attached to the Tau Cross (symbol of forgiveness) which means that because of their willful submission to spiritual thinking (symbolized by water), they are pardoned of all past errors. The man's legs are in the form of the Tau Cross (if you lock at him right side up). This reminds us that he is a willing victim (willingly trains his mind to think in reverse of the masses). His hands are behind his back, which means he has ceased from the mass form of actions in life, and acts in a hidden level unperceived by the average world.

The Sealed Magical Book of Moses

NUN - Death. Psalm 119: 105-112
Nun means fish.

The reason that the word "fish" was chosen to correspond to this card is because the fish is an esoteric symbol for change. Another word for death is transition or change. Nothing ever really dies-it only changes form. The figure of the skeleton of death riding on a white horse not a symbol of evil; this card is symbolic of the death of old destructive ideas and beliefs. The dead king with his crown removed from his head is symbolic of the rule of the carnal consciousness, being the first thing that must die.

The child and the woman kneel, and the woman looks away. This is symbolic of the death of childish pettiness or spiritual immaturity. The woman looking away is symbolic of the subconscious mind having to let go of destructive ideas that have been programmed into it by repetition, over a long period of error. She looks away because she does not wish to face death. The subconscious mind is reluctant, at first, to release old habits and ideas. The bishop stands, praying for mercy, symbolic of the fact that the last thing to die is a person's false religious convictions. These false concepts are the most difficult to dispose of. In the background is the Sun, rising between two pillars or towers. The rising Sun is symbolic of the truth that with change come the resurrection of a new life. The towers are symbolic of harmony between the two mental levels, conscious and subconscious.

The white flower on the black flag is a version of the Rose and Cross, and reveals that we must die out to the limitation of human existence so that we may resurrect to state of purification. There are three layers of five petals, each which reveal that by the purification of our five senses we also purify our physical, emotional and mental vehicles. Another interesting thought about the word "Nun" is that Joshua was called the son of Nun. The Hebrew name of Joshua means deliverer. He was the helper of Moses, and when Moses died he took over the task of leading Israel to the promised land. The Greek name that corresponds to Joshua is Jesus. With the passing of the first law (the death of Moses), Joshua took over the great task. With the dawning of a new age (the Age of Pisces-the fish), Jesus was the deliverer to initiate true seekers of the path to a higher state of awareness (the Promised Land). It is no accident that Nun means fish and that Jesus the Christ (Joshua in Hebrew) began his work at the dawn of the age of Pisces (the Fish). The symbol of the fish represented change-the introduction of the New Covenant.

SAMECH - Temperance Psalm 119: 113-120
Samech means support.

On this card we behold a mighty angel pouring water from one cup into another. This is symbolic of harmony and a flowing unity between our conscious and subconscious levels of mental awareness (the cups being symbols of these levels). The water is symbolic of spiritual thought. The angel is symbolic of the superconscious level of awareness, which, at this stage of development is in control of the other levels of mind. On the angel's forehead is a golden circle, which reveals the opening of the third eye. On his chest is a white square with a golden triangle that reveals purity of life within the kingdom of the four elements, and the revelation of our individual trinity as body, mind and spirit. In addition, the four sides of the square and the three sides of the triangle add up to seven that is a sacred number. The angel stands with one foot in water, and the other on land-another symbol for balance between our physical and spiritual sides of nature. We experience support from higher realms of life when we use temperance or create balance between our physical and spiritual selves.

AYIN - The Devil Psalm 119: 121-128
Ayin means eye.

Evil is a reality that exists and endures only by the energy it receives from man's negative thoughts, emotions and deeds. One may ask why the word 'eye' is connected to this card. The answer is that man sees things in a distorted consciousness. In other words,, he misinterprets what he sees so as to be in a condition of error. The word 'evil' spelled backwards is 'live'. The word devil spelled backwards is 'lived'. This reveals that most people live or have lived life backwards. There is an old saying: "believe only half of what you see". Most of us, even after having attained a certain degree of development, may still be confused about the appearance of things. The Greek word for devil is 'diabolos', meaning one who lies and throws blocks in the way. I wish to call your attention to an unusual correspondence: In the card of The Lovers the man and woman stand in front of trees with the angel of the High Self between them. Notice that in the card of The Devil, the trees have transformed into tails on the man and woman. This is symbolic of falling back into erroneous sense consciousness, or negative ways. They have horns, symbolic of misuse of thought. Around their necks are chains that bind them to the seat of the devil and this reveals misuse of the spoken word (the word come through the throat). The devil represents the misapplied power of higher consciousness. At the top of the devil's head is the inverted pentagram (the five pointed star upside down). The pentagram is a symbol for the Christed man when the one point is pointing up. But when inverted, it becomes the symbol of antichrist, or the misuse of the Universal Life Force. We can sum up the meaning of this card as a warning not to misuse the power of our development. The student must be aware of the possibilities of falling back into negative ways. A person may advance to a great degree on the path, then find themselves going through inner conflicts and problems in everyday life. They will, at this point, be tempted to think, speak and act in a negative manner. The person may even slip and fall back for a time. However, it is very important that one does not remain in this condition. We must realize the illusion of evil and force ourselves out of its grip.

The Sealed Magical Book of Moses

PEH - The Tower Psalm 119: 129-136
Peh means mouth.

In our consideration of the last card (the devil) we realized how old negative habits may try to reassert themselves. This card of The Tower gives the same revelation in a different- way. The tower is symbolic of the "Tower of Babel"(confusion). There are elements of consciousness within us, which try to force their way into a state of harmony without giving up their grip on negativity. This is revealed in the story of the Tower of Babel, as recorded in the eleventh chapter of the Book of Genesis. The people tried to build a tower to heaven. The tower is symbolic of the illusions of the false ego. It is said that God destroyed the tower and the people were scattered. In this card, the people are symbolic of negative cell consciousness and false concepts. The lightening (the High Self) strikes the tower, casting down its crown (false mental concepts) and the people (negative cell consciousness). Around one person is twelve flames; around the other are ten flames. This totals twenty-two, and is symbolic of overcoming our negative hindrances through consideration of the twenty-two keys of life (which you are considering in this lesson). The word mouth is connected with this card because we achieve this victory over negativity through the power of the spoken word, or by dynamic affirmations of positive faith.

TZADDI - The Star Psalm 119: 137-144
Tzaddi means fish hook.

The Superconscious mind appears as a woman in this card. She has her right foot in the water (symbolic of spiritual thought), and kneeling on her left knee upon dry ground. She pours water from two pitchers (symbolic of the conscious and subconscious). This resembles the card of Temperance, and the scene reveals the principle of balance. From the pitcher in her left hand she pours water on the earth and the water breaks up into five streams, symbolic of the purified five senses. From the pitcher in her right hand she pours water into a larger body of water, symbolic of the purified subconscious mind contributing a portion of its developed wisdom to the mass consciousness, or universal subconscious mind. There is a tree in the background that breaks out into three main branches, symbolic of the mind, divided into three levels-yet one, as the three branches come from one trunk. Above the tree is a bird, believed to be the legendary Phoenix-symbol of regeneration. There are seven small eight-pointed stars, which represent the awakened seven psychic centers within man. In the center is a large eight-pointed star, symbolic of us reaching a state of unity with all levels of our being. The eight-pointed star is a symbol of regeneration and immortality. I also wish to mention that her knee upon the earth is symbolic of the virtue of humility in our life. The term 'fish hook' is connected to this card because it reveals that by developing the qualities illustrated in the card, we may capture the fish (another symbol for Christ) for our own. These twenty-two symbols reveal the same story of human searching for answers to life's mysteries. The same truths are revealed repeatedly through different symbols, until they impregnate all levels of consciousness. Now, let us consider the next card.

KOPH - The Moon Psalm 119: 145-152
Koph means back of the head.

The moon has a bright side and a dark side. As it rotates we see, at one point, half of the bright and half of the dark; this we call a half moon. When the dark side faces us, it becomes invisible, yet it is there. As we contemplate the cycles of the moon in a mystic way, we realize that darkness is often symbolic of the hidden wisdom in the studies of occultism (the word 'occult' means something that is hidden). Around the moon on the card are thirty two rays of light, symbolic of the Thirty-Two Paths of Wisdom, as embodied in the twenty two cards that we are considering and the Ten Emanations of God (I reveal the Ten Manifestations of God in the first chapter of my book "The Final Solution"). Ancient mystics illustrated the Thirty-Two Paths of Wisdom in a symbol called "The Tree of Life". Therefore, this card reveals that by comprehension of the Tree of Life we awaken the dynamic potentials within the hidden chamber (back of the head) of our inner mind. The moon is symbolic of our intuitive faculties or subconscious mind.

The two pillars in this card represent balance between the seen and the unseen: in the foreground is the seen, and in the background is the unseen (illustrated by the mountains). Prom the water (the Universal Consciousness) a lobster emerges. This is symbolic of having a firm grip on both sides of life (the seen and the unseen). The grass is symbolic of development within our physical existence. A bright path leads from the water to the mountains, symbolic of the spiritual path within. On one side of the path is the wolf (a symbol of the devil, or the blocks which sometimes hinder our spiritual progress), and on the other side is a dog (the dog is a symbol of God's power, present with us in physical life). The dog has been called man's best friend.

In esoteric teachings, wisdom is sometimes cloaked in obvious symbolism: the reason some teachers use a dog as a symbol of the God-Power is simple: The word 'dog' spelled backwards is God. Under the moon are fifteen flames. When you add 1 + 5 you get 6, symbolic of the six days of creation. When you have done your best in developing your full potential you can look forward to the seventh day of rest, when you look upon all the things you have become through your sincere efforts, and see that it is good. There is something else that I wish to point out about the dog and the wolf. Both of them look, and appear to be howling at the moon. This reveals that all experiences contribute towards the awakening of our inner mind. Bad events can be blessings in disguise for they prompt us to pray more and try harder. The positive events give us the added energy and reward for our efforts.

The Sealed Magical Book of Moses

RESH - The Sun Psalm 119: 153-160
Resh means face.

As the moon is symbolic of the awakened inner mind, the sun is symbolic of illuminated reason in the conscious mind. The moon has no light of its own but reflects the light of the sun. What this means is that we make conscious effort towards selfmastery, and as we do so the spiritual thinking of our conscious mind will shine and reflect on our subconscious. As these two levels of our mental awareness work in harmony they eliminate negativity from our lives. The word Resh means face or front of the head (the word corresponding to the moon meant back of the head). Resh means the conscious awareness that we are most familiar with. Since the card of the Sun corresponds to this word, we see that it reveals the glorified or illuminated conscious awareness. On this card the sun has a human face which is a clue that you are to picture your face within the sun. The child on the card is symbolic of reaching a state of the new birth or a transformed life. "Except ye be converted, and become as little children, ye shall not enter into the kingdom of heaven" St. Matthew 18:3

On the child's head are six circles, symbolic of the purified five senses and the awakened sixth sense. The feather rising from the child's head represents the awakened cosmic fire of the Holy Spirit. The child sits on horse, symbolic of soberness and tranquility. There are eight layers of masonry upon which are four sunflowers: this symbol reveals that by uniting that which is below with that which is above we develop our power within the four worlds, or realms of existence (Physical, astral or emotional, mental and spiritual). Notice that three of the sunflowers are grouped together-they represent the astral, mental and spiritual worlds. The sunflower by itself to the right represents the physical world. Notice that a flag or banner on a pole comes between this sunflower and the other. This reveals that there is a veil of mystery which separates the seen from the unseen. However, we also notice that the child has his hand on the flagpole, and this reveals that the spiritually minded person may lift the veil and see beyond.

SHIN - The Judgment Psalm 119: 161-168.
Shin means tooth.

When an infant begins to develop, it starts cutting teeth. The tooth, causing a great deal of soreness to the gum, emerges (resurrects) and becomes an important faculty of taking food into the body. Remember-Shin means tooth. In the judgment card we behold the scene of the resurrection; this is the resurrection of the righteous because the people raise their hands in welcome and praise. Notice that the coffins float on water. This reveals that by spiritual thought we resurrect the hidden spiritual qualities of our being; they have been hindered (as though dead in a coffin), but now they are free (resurrected). There is a man, a woman and a child in both the foreground and the background of the scene. This is symbolic of the illuminated conscious mind (father), the illuminated subconscious mind (mother), and the transformed (reborn) personality (child). The pair of trinities reveal that this awakening (resurrection) is taking place in both the physical and spiritual sides of life. There are white mountains, indicating that we are arising into higher realms of consciousness. The angel Gabriel blows his trumpet, symbolic of the "Clarion Call" to ascend into higher consciousness. On his trumpet is a flag with a cross, revealing that we may achieve victory over death (illusion) even while in the physical world.

TAU - The World Psalm 119: 169-176.
Tau means mark or cross.

In the center of this card, the figure appears to be dancing with legs arranged like the hanged man. The lady is clothed with a violet loin cloth, symbolic of control of the veil that separates the seen from the unseen. She holds two wands of light, symbolic of balance between the conscious and subconscious mind. A wreath surrounds her. symbolic of the circle of eternity: the number of The Pool is 0 as he represents the eternal past, when man left the high place and descended into lower realms. The person in the card of The World represents the regenerated person, now living within the Lav of the eternal circle from which he departed, and has now returned. In the four corners of the card are the symbols of the four elements. The legs form the Tau Cross, and the upper and lower binding on the wreath form and early sign of the Cross. These reveal the hidden and mysterious symbol of the Rosy Cross, for out of the cross (the limitation of physical existence), the Rose (the True Self) emerges.

Frequent meditation upon the 22 symbolic cards and the corresponding letters of the Hebrew Alphabet (the 22 words of power), will bring an inner awakening to the consciousness of the faithful student. You will discover for yourself by personal practice that these cards contain the symbolic keys of the Book of Thoth. It is wise to read the prescribed verses of the 119th. Psalm for each card before you meditate on the card.

The illustrations on the cards are symbolic of states of conscious through which we pass in the quest for self-discovery and mastery. Therefore, visualize yourself in the cards, acting out the drama of unfoldment in your imagination. We use our conscious mind to look at the cards, but the symbols register on the subconscious, and eventually our reflections awaken our higher mind to an advanced degree. I suggest that you use these symbols according to the instructions in this chapter three times before doing the following talismanic work, for better results.

3. INSTRUCTIONS FOR MOSES' MAGICAL ART

What follows are simple instructions for working with the Magic of Moses intended for the student who wishes to use this power to improve his or her life. It is not necessary to perform the complicated ceremonial rituals described in the texts rendered by magicians of the middle ages. Such rituals are only used by individuals who may not be pure in their intentions, therefore they take great care to protect themselves, as such people must invoke negative spirits to fulfill their selfish designs.

What I teach is the sacred magical work which a person of pure intention may perform in a simple manner. My teaching in the first part of this book was to purify and prepare you for this special work, and you will be working with positive spirits of God. Follow these instructions and you will feel a wonderful power being liberated from within you. This power will help you in many ways. The following rituals are simple yet powerful, practical yet sacred. Treat them with reverence and secrecy. To speak of these things to people who do not believe is a waste of time and energy. Furthermore, your work will be more effective if you keep it a secret. Others may hinder you if they know too much of your work. Your secrecy will be the key to your advancement and magnetic personal power.

THE BEST TIME FOR THIS WORK:

The most important time to observe in this work is that you must absolutely do this only during the seven days before a full Moon or at the time of the full Moon. Other than this, you may perform your ritual work at any time of the day that will afford you uninterrupted privacy. However, it is best to do this work between midnight and dawn as this is a quiet period of time. The most important thing is to work at the time which is best for you. The only thing I insist upon is that you observe the full Moon period already mentioned.

SPIRITUAL PREPARATION:

Thirteen days of preparation sire required before starting this work. The thirteen day period should be just before the full Moon period so you will not have to wait until the following month. Your spiritual preparation require doing the following things:

1. Prepare an alter. This does not have to be an elaborate alter; it can be the top of a dresser, table or desk where you will work. You will place the required items on the alter when you are performing your work, then put them away when you are finished (unless you live alone and can set up a permanent alter). This area must be clean. The important thing is to build your magnetic energy into that area during this thirteen day preparation. Each day you are to devote at least fifteen to thirty minutes at your alter. I will teach you what to do during this time, but first we will consider how the alter should be arranged. Secure and prepare the following items as follows.

The Sealed Magical Book of Moses

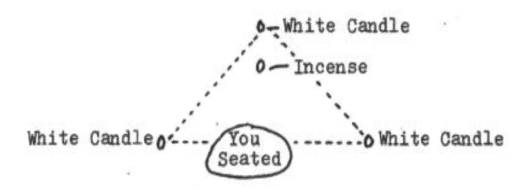

You can buy the white candles at any local variety or candle shop. The best incense to use is powdered sandlewood, Temple Incense or my own special blend called "Moses Incense".

You will also need to prepare a special Holy Water in the following manner: Place some spring or mineral water in a clean jar. Add one tablespoon each of the following three herbs; Hyssop, Sacred Bark and Laurel. Close the Jar (you will use this water during the thirteen days of preparation and every time you do your work so be sure you have enough-about one quart). Have your medallion containing the secret name of Moses ready to consecrate during the period of preparation.

2. Each day for thirteen days, perform the following ritual for fifteen to thirty minutes: light the candles and incense-turn all other lights off so there is only the soft light of the candles in the room. Choose the time of day or night that is best for you. Only make sure it is during a time when you will not be disturbed (it may be wise to take the phone off the hook).

Take several deep breaths while you place your hands around the jar of herbal water. Focus your attention on the jar for several moments, then the incense, and finally the candles. Then use your imagination to form the following mental image of yourself. Visualize yourself approaching a golden alter in a beautiful white marble temple. See the Three Wisemen standing to your left, then repeat these words out loud:

"Oh Caspar, Blessed Be. Oh Melchior, Blessed Be. Oh Balthasar, Blessed Be".

After you have said these words, imagine that Moses now appears to your right in the Temple of light, and you suddenly become aware that a glorious light surrounds you. Then close this book and place it on the alter in front of you. Then place a copy of the Holy Bible on top of this book. Open the Bible to the 91st. Psalm and read it out loud. As you read the Psalm, hold the Holy Shemmah Medallion between your palms. This will conclude your preparation ritual. This same ritual is to be done each day for the thirteen days of preparation.

The Sealed Magical Book of Moses

PERFORMING THE MAGICAL WORK:

Remember, you must only do your work during the seven days before a full Moon or any day of the full Moon. Take note of the following steps of this work.

1. Set up your alter.
2. Have a closed Bible on the alter in front of you.

3. Take the bottle of Holy Water which you have prepared and meditated with during the thirteen day period. Shake it well. Open the jar and pour a little of the water in your left palm, then rub your hands together (as if washing them).Next, apply a small amount of the water to the Shemmah Medallion-then place this medallion around your neck (as stated earlier, it will enhance your work to wear this blessed medallion that contains the secret name of Moses).

4. Apply some of the water to the four comers of the magical circle seal (Seal #1 - see the centerfold) as illustrated in figure #1. You will use this seal with all the other seals: After you anoint the four corners of this seal you are to place it on the Bible, then you would place the particular seal you may be working with on top of the magical circle.

FIGURE #1. THE MAGICAL CIRCLE SEAL (all seals must be placed on this seal during the activating ritual).

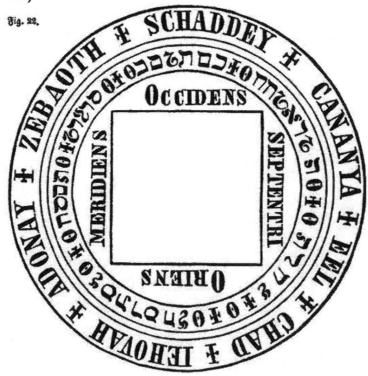

5. Light the special incense and the candles. You are now ready to activate the power and invoke the spirit of the seal of your choice. The balance of this chapter describes and illustrates the most popular legendary seals of Moses' Magical Art. We also give the formulas (prayers) for activating the seal and how to use it afterwards.

"When you have chosen one or more seals that you wish to use you may cut them out of the centerfold provided with this book. However, you can only place one seal at a time on the Magical Circle Seal in figure #1. So, if you wish to activate more than cne seal during a session, place one seal on the circle, do the required activating ritual then put that seal aside and go to the next seal. Keep this book near by so you can refer to the activating formula for your chosen seal(s). When you have finished, put all the items away and go about your daily affairs.

6. Apply the water to the four corners of your chosen seal before placing it on top of seal #1. Now, consider the following seal with their magical virtues.

FIGURE #2 Seal of the Ministering Archangels.

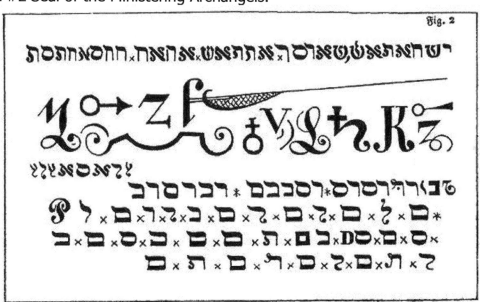

The true and glorious secret of this seal is that it can bring to the surface all the hidden treasures of wisdom within us to multiply our resources for physical prosperity. After you have activated its power, place it in an envelope and tape it on a hidden part of your basement wall. If you do not have a basement or live in an apartment, then tape the envelope underneath your favorite chair.

Here is the prayer (formula) to activate this seal:

"I (say your first and last name), a servant of God, call upon the Ministering Archangels that they compel the beings of water, fire, air and earth to help me. In the name of the Almighty God, may all creatures of the elements bring me the wisdom of my hidden resources with the help of the Archangels".

FIGURE #3 SEAL OF THE CHOIR HOSTS.

This is also called the Seal of the highest Good Fortune. The secret of this seal is that it should be carried on one's person after it is activated. Here is the prayer to activate this seal:

"I (your first and last name) call upon thee, angelic choir hosts, to guide me into actions which will bring me good fortune. Amen".

FIGURE #4 SEAL OF THE MINISTERING THRONE ANGELS.

The secret of this seal is that it gives its user the blessing of. being beloved, and giving power over one's enemies. Here is the prayer to activate this seal:

"In the Name of God Almighty, I (your first and last name), call upon the Archangels, Michael, Gabriel, Raphael and Uriel to help me through the administration of the Throne Angels. May I be beloved, and may I gain victory over all enemies seen and unseen. So be it". (this seal is also to be carried on one's person).

FIGURE #5 SEAL OF MINISTERING CHERUBIM AND SERAPHIM.

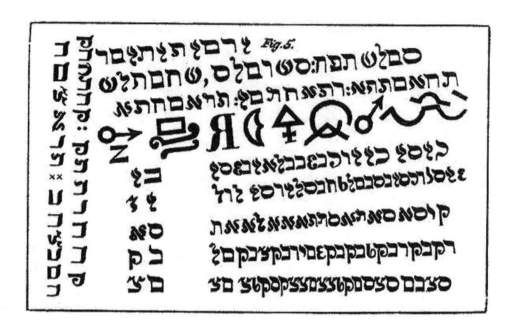

It is believed that for one to carry this seal brings the blessing of a long life.

Here is the prayer to activate this seal:

"I (your first and last name), a servant of God, Invoke your help oh spirits of long life. May you bless me with the Wisdom of Solomon to do the things which will extend my life. In the Name of the Universal Cosmic Mind".

FIGURE #6 SEAL OF THE ANGELS OF POWER.

The great secret of this seal is that it helps a person who carries it to stay healthy and overcome illness if their time of departure has not come. Here is the prayer to activate this seal:

"I (your first and last name) invoke the spirits of good health, by the glorious power that manifested in the flesh of Jesus the Christ, to bless me with physical power against illness. Thank you. So Mote it Be".

FIGURE #7 SEAL OF THE POWER ANGELS.

This seal compels the angels and spirits of the elements to help you by the authority of the power angels. If placed under one's pillow, it believed to help the person receive direction and inspiration through dreams. It is wise to seal this talisman in laminating plastic (which you can obtain at a stationary or variety store) so it will not be damaged by keeping it under your pillow over a long period of time. Here is the prayer to activate this seal:

"I (your first and last name), a servant of God, invoke the holy messengers to give me guidance through my dreams. Fiat, Fiat, Fiat".

FIGURE #8 SEAL OF THE MOST OBEDIENT ANGELS OF THE SEVEN PLANETS.

It is known by Adepts that it helps us to realize our full potential (brings forth the hidden treasures of the mines). If placed on the floor under one's bed, it will help us wake up refreshed and filled with healthy expectation for the new day. Here is the prayer to activate this seal:

"I (your first and last name), a servant of God, call upon the holy spirits of the planets to help me live in harmony with nature that I may realize my full potential. Amen".

The Magical Circle Seal and the seven seals we have just considered form the first part of this work. The seals and rituals in the next chapter form the more advanced work.

WHY ARE THE TALISMANIC SEALS EFFECTIVE?:

In the work of the Magical Art of Moses one accomplishes his desires with the help of advanced spirits. The original angelic teachers of the Cabala wished to give man the means to communicate with higher "beings of nature and the cosmos, without the limited language of humanity. This is where the Language of Symbolism comes in: profane human communication can never persuade the advanced spirits to serve us. Only pure communication from a sincere heart can touch the higher cosmic forces, and that pure communication is embodied in the holy talismans and seals under consideration. They help us focus that communication of unspeakable language from within that reaches from earth to heaven.

PERSONALIZE YOUR SEALS:

After you activate the power of your chosen seal(s), write your name on the back. This will help focus your faith for the desired results to' manifest.

PRESERVE YOUR SEALS:

It is good to seal your talismans in laminating plastic which you can purchase in your local stationary store. This will protect them from where and soiling with the passing of time. It is also wise to re-apply the holy water to the four corners of each seal every month to keep them blessed with the high rate of vibration you generated when first activating it.

WHERE TO KEEP YOUR SEALS:

Seal #1. (the Magical Circle Seal) should be kept in a secret place with your other alter items.

The seals which you have activated should be carried with you. As already said, it is best to seal them in laminating plastic for protection, but you must also keep them together: most people keep the seals in a red flannel bag, other wrap them in a clean handkerchief and pin it closed. The important thing is that you keep your chosen seals on your person.

Any seals which you have not chosen to activate should be kept in a secret place with your alter items.

Do not allow any other person to see or touch your seals. If that should happen, you will have to activate them again.

I suggest that you work with the seals outlined in this chapter for a few weeks before proceeding with the seals of the advanced work that we will consider in the final section of this work.

4. ADVANCED WORK

The following seals should be activated the same as the others. However, there is a difference in the prayer to activate the seal; it is not spoken but is to be written on the back of the seal under your name. There will be from one to three words to activate each seal. These words represent hidden names of God, angelic hosts and spirits of the elements. In other words, after you apply the holy water to the four corner of your chosen seal, you then place it on top of the magical circle seal (see figure #1) while you meditate on your desire. Finally turn the seal over and write your name on the back of it, then write the special word or name of power that activates the seal, under your name.

FIGURE #9. SEAL OF RAB CALEB DOCTOR ORIENTAL.

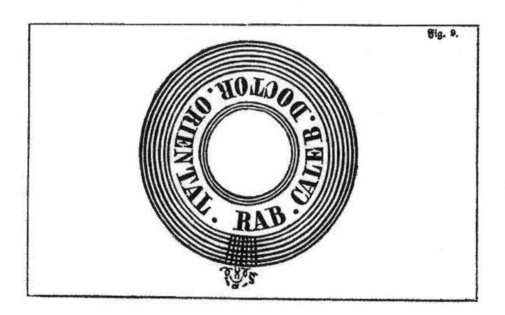

In this work, the word 'Oriental' means hidden or inner, while 'Occidental' means outer. Therefore, this seal means the Inner Doctor. With the help of the inner doctor through this seal, it is said that one can maintain health of mind and body by touching his forehead, heart and feet with this seal, and then hold it in both hands. This is to be done as often as possible. The activating word is "RA".

FIGURE #10. FIRST TABLE OF THE SPIRITS OF THE AIR (SYLPHS).

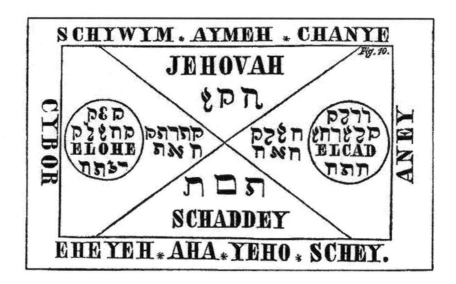

These nature spirits give the ability to think quickly. Keep this with you. Activating word is "PARALDA".

FIGURE #11. SECOND TABLE OF THE SPIRITS OF FIRE (SALAMANDERS).

These nature spirits give emotional blessings and magnetism. Keep this with you. The activating word is "DJIN".

FIGURE #12. THIRD TABLE OF THE SPIRITS OF WATER (UNDINES).

These nature spirits give one the blessing of philosophical thought. Keep with you. Activating word is "NECKSA".

FIGURE #13. FOURTH TABLE OF THE SPIRITS OF THE EARTH (GNOMES).

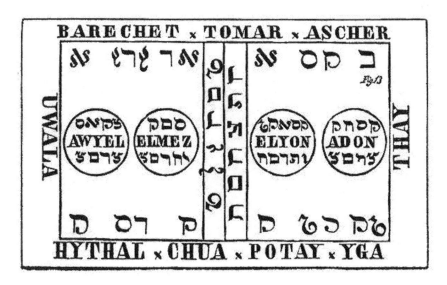

These nature spirits give one help in earthly matters, such as business and finance. The activating word is "GOB".

FIGURE #14. FIFTH TABLE OF THE SPIRITS OF SATURN.

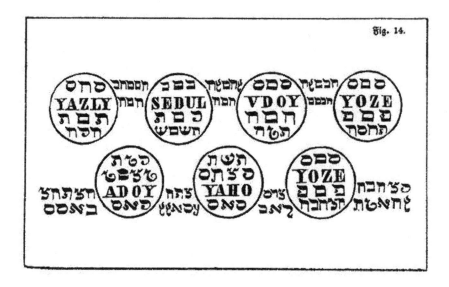

The spirits of this seal are believed to bring us good luck in games of chance. Activating words are "JEHOVAH, YAHWEY".

FIGURE #15. SIXTH TABLE OF THE SPIRITS OF JUPITER.

The spirits of this seal help in legal matters. Activating words "MOSES, ELION".

The Sealed Magical Book of Moses

FIGURE #16. SEVENTH TABLE OF THE SPIRITS OF MARS.

The spirits of this seal help to reconcile those who have quarreled. Activating words are "AARON, ANEPOBEIJARON".

FIGURE #17. EIGHTH TABLE OF THE SPIRITS OF THE SUN.

The spirits of this seal are said to help one attain honor and wealth. The Activating word is "ZEBAOTH".

FIGURE #18. NINTH TABLE OF THE SPIRITS OF VENUS.

The spirits of this seal make one beloved and helps in matters of the h e a r t through dreams and intuition. It also helps one gain favor in business. Activating words are "AWEL, GOD, TETRAGRAMATON".

FIGURE #19. TENTH TABLE OF THE SPIRITS OF MERCURY.

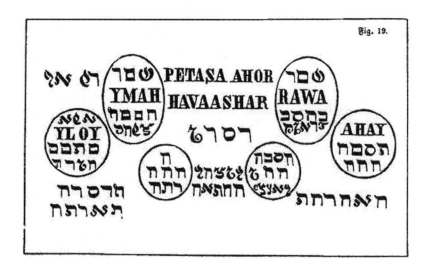

The spirits of this seal help us to formulate plans. Activating words is "ADONAI"

FIGURE #20. ELEVENTH TABLE OF THE SPIRITS.

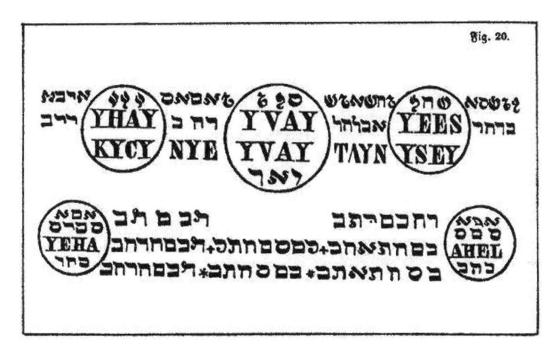

The spirits of guidance work through this seal to bring good fortune to the one who keeps it with him. If you wish direct communication with these spirits you must use this seal with the twelfth table. Activating word for this seal is "AGLA"

FIGURE #21. TWELFTH TABLE OF SCHEMHAM-FORASCH.

The word Schemhamforasch represents the 72 holy Names of God. The ancients taught that when God created the universe he spoke a sacred word that embodied 72 aspects of his being. The original word is hidden, but the word 'Schemhamforasch' is symbolic of that word. If you wish complete communication with holy spirits hold this seal often while you meditate. They will appear to you in a dream, vision or in some manner. Hold it in your right hand. If you desire intense communication with the spirit of good fortune (see eleventh table - figure 20), place this seal on top of that seal and hold them both in your right hand. Activating words for this seal are "PROCUL ESTE FROFANI".

There are other legendary talismans of Moses' Magical Art, some of which give the same results as those presented here, while others have not come down to us with a pure formula for activating them. However, in this work I have attempted to provide the reader with a workable program of this art, which can be applied to daily life without the severity of advanced magical training.

Work faithfully with these wonderful secret and they will unlock the door to the Grand Tempi of Magic within you.

BLESSED BE

EXCLUSIVE BONUS MATERIAL ADDED TO THIS VOLUME

THE ATTENDING ANGELS AND THE DEATH OF MOSES

God tells Moses several times that it is time to die: "Go up unto this mountain of Abarim and see the land which I have given to the people of Israel. And when you have seen it, be gathered to your fathers as your brother Aaron was gathered."[1]
• "Behold the time has come for you to die."[2]
• "Behold now you will sleep with your fathers."[3]
• "Ascend this mountain of the Abarim, Mt. Nebo... and view the land of Canaan, which I am giving to the people of Israel as a possession; and die on the mount which you ascend and be gathered to your ancestors."[4]

The Death of Moses
By Alexandre Cabanel, mid 19th century

At least on one occasion Moses appears to have protested God's decree that he die before entering the land of Canaan. Moses reflects how he had beseeched God to let him "see the good land beyond the Jordan" but the Lord had been angry and refused.[5]

Writes Bible scholar James Kugel: "These and yet other references suggested to some [early] interpreters that Moses might not in fact have been so eager to accept the divine decree. Perhaps, on the contrary, God's repeated instructions to Moses to die indicated that Moses was unwilling."[6] The writers of the midrash convey this reluctance through the recurring theme of angels dispatched to bring about Moses' death or to take charge of his soul after death, and Moses' interaction with them. Of the many such legends in Louis Ginzberg's classic work, "Legends of the Bible," the following two are representative.[7]

When the people and their leaders heard these words of Moses, they broke out into mournful weeping, and in the Tabernacle with bitter tears they entreated God to answer Moses' prayer, so that their cries rose even to the Throne of Glory. But then one hundred and eighty four myriads of angels under the leadership of the great angels Zakun and Lahash descended and snatched away the words of the suppliants, that they might not reach God. The angel Lahash indeed tried to restore to their place the words which the other angels had snatched away, so that they might reach God, but when Samael learned of this, he fettered Lahash with chains of fire and brought him before God, where he received sixty blows of fire and was expelled from the inner chamber of God because, contrary to God's wish, he had attempted to aid Moses in the fulfilment of his desire. When Israel now saw how the angels dealt with their prayers, they went to Moses and said, "The angels will not let us pray for you."

THE ANGEL OF DEATH SEEKS MOSES

When Moses saw that neither the world nor mankind could aid him, he betook himself to the Angel of the Face, to whom he said, "Pray for me, that God may take pity upon me, and that I may not die." But the angel replied: "Why, Moses, why do you exert yourself in vain? Standing behind the curtain that is drawn before the Lord, I heard that your prayer in this instance is not to be answered." Moses now laid his hand upon his head and wept bitterly, saying, "To whom shall I now go, that he might implore God's mercy for me?" God was now very angry with Moses because he would not resign himself to the doom that had been sealed, but His wrath vanished as soon as Moses spoke the words: "The Lord, the Lord, a God full of compassion and gracious, slow to anger, and plenteous in mercy and truth; keeping mercy for thousands, forgiving iniquity and transgression and sin."

"I want to know," God asked him, "why you are so much aggrieved at your impending death." Moses replied: "I am afraid of the sword of the Angel of Death." God: "If this is the reason then speak no more in this matter, for I will not deliver you into his hand." Moses, however, would not yield, but furthermore said, "Shall my mother Jochebed, to whom my life brought so much grief, suffer sorrow after my death also?" God: "So was it in My mind even before I created the world, and so is the course of the world; every generation has its learned men, every generation has its leaders, every generation has its guides. Up to now it was your duty to guide the people, but now the time is ripe for your disciple Joshua to relieve you of the office destined for him."

Death of Moses on Mount Nebo

With God descended from heaven three angels, Michael, Gabriel and Zagzagel. Gabriel arranged Moses' couch. Michael spread upon it a purple garment, and Zagzagel laid down a woolen pillow. God stationed Himself over Moses' head, Michael to his right, Gabriel to his left, and Zagzagel at his feet, whereupon God addressed Moses: "Cross your feet," and Moses did so. He then said, "Fold your hands and lay them upon your breast," and Moses did so. Then God said, "Close thine eyes," and Moses did so.

Then God spoke to Moses' soul: "My daughter, one hundred and twenty years had I decreed that you should dwell in this righteous man's body, but hesitate not now to leave it, for your time is run." ...But the soul replied: "Lord of the world! I desire to remain with this righteous man; for whereas the two angels Azza and Azazel when they descended from heaven to earth, corrupted their way of life and loved the daughters of the earth, so that in punishment You suspended them between heaven and earth, the son of Amram, a creature of flesh and blood, from the day upon which You revealed Yourself from the bush of thorns, has lived apart from his wife. Let me therefore remain where I am."

When Moses saw that his soul refused to leave him, he said to her: "Is this because the Angel of Death wishes to show his power over you?" The soul replied: "Nay, God does not wish to deliver me into the hands of death." Moses: "Will you, perchance, weep when the others will weep at my departure?" The soul: "The Lord has delivered mine eyes from tears.'" Moses: "Will you, perchance, go into Hell when I am dead?" The soul: " I will walk before the Lord in the land of the living." When Moses heard these words, he permitted his soul to leave him, saying to her: "Return unto your rest, O my soul; for the Lord hath dealt bountifully with thee." God thereupon took Moses' soul by kissing him upon the mouth.

Moses' activity did not, however, cease with his death, for in heaven he is one of the servants of the Lord. God buried Moses' body in a spot that remained unknown even to Moses himself. Only this is known concerning it, that a subterranean passage connects it with the graves of the Patriarchs. Altough Moses' body lies dead in its grave, it is still as fresh as when he was alive.

[1] **Numbers 27:12**
[2] **Deut. 31:14**
[3] **Deut. 31:16**
[4] **Deut. 32:49-50**
[5] **Deut. 3:23-27**
[6] **James L. Kugel, The Bible as It Was (Cambridge, MA: Harvard University Press, 1997)**
[7] **Louis Ginzberg, Legends of the Bible (Philadelphia: Jewish Publication Society, 1956), pp. 485-502**

THE HISTORY OF MOSES' MAGICAL ROD

When Adam and Eve went forth from Paradise, Adam, as if knowing that he was never to return to his place, cut off a branch from the tree of good and evil, which is the fig-tree, and took it with him and went forth; and it served him as a staff all the days of his life. After the death of Adam, his son Seth took it, for there were no weapons as yet at that time. This rod was passed on from hand to hand unto Noah, and from Noah to Shem; and it was handed down from Shem to Abraham as a blessed thing from the Paradise of God.

With this rod Abraham broke the images and graven idols which his father made, and therefore God said to him, 'Get thee out of thy father's house,' etc. It was in his hand in every country as far as Egypt, and from Egypt to Palestine. Afterwards Isaac took it, and (it was handed down) from Isaac to Jacob; with it he fed the flocks of Laban the Aramean in Paddan Aram. After Jacob Judah his fourth son took it; and this is the rod which Judah gave to Tamar his daughter-in-law, with his signet ring and his napkin, as the hire for what he had done. From him (it came) to Pharez. At that time there were wars everywhere, and an angel took the rod, and laid it in the Cave of Treasures in the mount of Moab, until Midian was built.

There was in Midian a man, upright and righteous before God, whose name was Yathrô (Jethro). When he was feeding his flock on the mountain, he found the cave and took the rod by divine agency; and with it he fed his sheep until his old age. When he gave his daughter to Moses, he said to him, 'Go in, my son, take the rod, and go forth to thy flock.' When Moses had set his foot upon the threshold of the door, an angel moved the rod, and it came out of its own free will towards Moses. And Moses took the rod, and it was with him until God spake with him on mount Sinai.

When God said to him, 'Cast the rod upon the ground,' he did so, and it became a great serpent; and the Lord said, 'Take it,' and he did so, and it became a rod as at first. This is the rod which God gave him for help and a deliverance; that it might be a wonder, and that with it he might deliver Israel from the oppression of the Egyptians. By the will of the living God this rod became a serpent in

Egypt. By it God spake to Moses; and it swallowed up the rod of Pôsdî the sorceress of the Egyptians. With it Moses smote the sea of Sôph in its length and breadth, and the depths congealed in the heart of the sea. It was in Moses' hands in the wilderness of Ashîmôn, and with it he smote the stony rock, and the waters flowed forth. Then God gave serpents power over the children of Israel to destroy them, because they had angered Him at the waters of strife. And Moses prayed before the Lord, and God said to him, 'Make thee a brazen serpent, and lift it up with the rod, and let the children of Israel look upon it and be healed.'

Moses did as the Lord had commanded him, and he placed the brazen serpent in the sight of all the children of Israel in the wilderness; and they looked upon it and were healed. After all the children of Israel were dead, save Joshua the son of Nun and Caleb the son of Yôphannâ (Jephunneh), they went into the promised land, and took the rod with them, on account of the wars with the Philistines and Amalekites. And Phineas hid the rod in the desert, in the dust at the gate of Jerusalem, where it remained until our Lord Christ was born. And He, by the will of His divinity, shewed the rod to Joseph the husband of Mary, and it was in his hand when he fled to Egypt with our Lord and Mary, until he returned to Nazareth.

From Joseph his son Jacob, who was surnamed the brother of our Lord, took it; and from Jacob Judas Iscariot, who was a thief, stole it. When the Jews crucified our Lord, they lacked wood for the arms of our Lord; and Judas in his wickedness gave them the rod, which became a judgment and a fall unto them, but an uprising unto many.

There were born to Moses two sons; the one called Gershom, which is interpreted 'sojourner;' and the other Eliezer, which is interpreted 'God hath helped me.' Fifty-two years after the birth of Moses, Joshua the son of Nun was born in Egypt. When Moses was eighty years old, God spake with him upon mount Sinai. And the cry of the children of Israel went up to God by reason of the severity of the oppression of the Egyptians; and God heard their groaning, and remembered His covenants with the fathers, Abraham, Isaac and Jacob, to whom He promised that in their seed should all nations be blessed. One day

The Sealed Magical Book of Moses

when Moses was feeding the flock of Jethro his father-in-law, the priest of Midian, he and the sheep went from the wilderness to mount Horeb, the mount of God; and the angel of the Lord appeared to him in a flame of fire in a bush, but the bush was not burnt. Moses said, 'I will turn aside and see this wonderful thing, how it is that the fire blazes in the bush, but the bush is not burnt.' God saw that he turned aside to look, and He called to him from within the bush, and said, 'Moses, Moses.' Moses said, 'Here am I, Lord.' God said to him, 'Approach not hither, for the place upon which thou standest is holy.' And God said to him, 'I am the God of Abraham, the God of Isaac, the God of Jacob;' and Moses covered his face, for he was afraid to look at Him.

Some say that when God spake with Moses, Moses stammered through fear. And the Lord said to him, 'I have seen the oppression of My people in Egypt, and have heard the voice of their cry, and I am come down to deliver them from the Egyptians, and to carry them up from that land to the land flowing with milk and honey; come, I will send thee to Egypt.'

Moses said, 'Who am I, Lord, that I should go to Pharaoh, and bring out those of the house of Israel from Egypt?' God said to him, 'I will be with thee.' Moses said to the Lord, 'If they shall say unto me, What is the Lord's name? what shall I say unto them?' God said, 'אֶהְיֶה אֲשֶׁר אֶהְיֶה', {Hebrew: AeHøYeH AaSheR AeHøYeH} that is, the Being who is the God of your fathers hath sent me to you. This is My name for ever, and this is My memorial to all generations.' God said to Moses, 'Go, tell Pharaoh everything I say to thee.' Moses said to the Lord, 'My tongue is heavy and stammers; how will Pharaoh accept my word?' God said to Moses, 'Behold, I have made thee a god to Pharaoh, and thy brother Aaron a phophet before thee; speak thou with Aaron, and Aaron shall speak with Pharaoh, and he shall send away the children of Israel that they may serve Me. And I will harden the heart of Pharaoh, and I will work My wonders in the land of Egypt, and will bring up My people the children of Israel from thence, and the Egyptians shall know that I am God.' And Moses and Aaron did everything that God had commanded them.

Moses was eighty-three years old when God sent him to Egypt. And God said to him, 'If Pharaoh shall seek a sign from thee, cast thy rod upon the ground, and it shall become a serpent.' Moses and Aaron came to Pharaoh, and threw down Moses' rod, and it became a serpent. The sorcerers of Egypt did the same1, but Moses' rod swallowed up those of the sorcerers; and the heart of Pharaoh was hardened, and he did not send away the people. And God wrought ten signs by the hands of Moses: first, turning the waters into blood; second, bringing up frogs upon them; third, domination of the gnats; fourth, noisome creatures of all kinds; fifth, the pestilence among the cattle; sixth, the plague of boils; seventh, the coming of hail-stones; eighth, the creation of locusts; ninth, the descent of darkness; tenth, the death of the firstborn.

When God wished to slay the first-born of Egypt, He said to Moses, 'This day shall be to you the first of months, that is to say, Nisan and the new year. On the tenth of this month, let every man take a lamb for his house, and a lamb for the house of his father; and if they be too few in number (for a whole lamb), let him and his neighbour who is near him share it. Let the lamb be kept until the fourteenth day of this month, and let all the children of Israel slay it at sunset, and let them sprinkle its blood upon the thresholds of their houses with the sign of the cross. This blood shall be to you a sign of deliverance, and I will see (it) and rejoice in you, and Death the destroyer shall no more have dominion over you;' and Moses and Aaron told the children of Israel all these things. And the Lord commanded them not to go out from their houses until morning; 'for the Lord will pass over the Egyptians to smite their firstborn, and will see the blood upon the thresholds, and will not allow the destroyer to enter their houses.'

When it was midnight, the Lord slew the firstborn of the Egyptians, from the firstborn of Pharaoh sitting upon his throne down to the last. And Pharaoh sent to Moses and Aaron, saying, 'Depart from among my people, and go, serve the Lord, as ye have said; and take your goods and chattels with you.' The Egyptians also urged the children of Israel to go forth from among them, through fear of death; and the children of Israel asked chains of gold and silver and costly clothing of the Egyptians, and spoiled them; and the Lord gave them favour in the sight of the Egyptians.

The children of Israel set out from Raamses to Succoth, six hundred thousand men; and when they entered Egypt in the days of Joseph, they were seventy-five souls in number. They remained in bodily and spiritual subjection four hundred and thirty years; from the day that God said to Abraham, 'Thy seed shall be a sojourner in the land of Egypt,' from that hour they were oppressed in their minds. When the people had gone out of Egypt on the condition that they should return, and did not return, Pharaoh pursued after them to bring them back to his slavery.

And they said to Moses, 'Why hast thou brought us out from Egypt? It was better for us to serve the Egyptians as slaves, and not to die here.' Moses said, 'Fear not, but see the deliverance which God will work for you to-day.' And the Lord said to Moses, 'Lift up thy rod and smite the sea, that the children of Israel may pass over as upon dry land.' And Moses smote the sea, and it was divided on this side and on that; and the children of Israel passed through the depth of the sea as upon dry land. When Pharaoh and his hosts came in after them, Moses brought his rod back over the sea, and the waters returned to their place; and all the Egyptians were drowned. And Moses bade the children of Israel to sing praises with the song 'Then sang Moses and the children of Israel' (Exod. xv. 1).

The children of Israel marched through the wilderness three days, and came to the place called Murrath (Marah) from the bitterness of its waters; and the people were unable to drink that water. And they lifted up their voice and murmured against Moses, saying, 'What shall we drink?' Moses prayed before God, and took absinth-wood, which is bitter in its nature, and threw it into the water, and it was made sweet.

There did the Lord teach them laws and judgments. And they set out from thence, and on the fifteenth of the second month, which is Îyâr, came to a place in which there were twelve wells and seventy palm-trees 1. Dâd-Îshô` says in his exposition of Paradise that the sorcerers Jannes and Jambres, who once opposed Moses, lived there. There was a well in that place, and over it was a bucket and brass chain; and devils dwelt there, because that place resembled Paradise. The blessed Mâkârîs (Macarius) visited that spot, but was unable to live there because of the wickedness of those demons; but that they might not boast over the human race, as if forsooth no one was able to live there, God commanded two anchorites, whose names no man knoweth, and they dwelt there until they died.

When the children of Israel saw that wilderness, they murmured against Moses, saying, 'It were better for us to have died in Egypt, being satisfied with bread, than to come forth into this arid desert for this people to perish by hunger.' And God said to Moses, 'Behold, I will bring manna down from heaven for you; a cloud shall shade you by day from the heat of the sun, and a pillar of fire shall give light before you by night.'

God said to Moses, 'Go up into this mountain, thou, and Aaron thy brother, and Nadab, and seventy chosen elders of the children of Israel, and let them worship from afar; and let Moses come near to Me by himself.' And they did as the Lord commanded them, and Moses drew near by himself, and the rest of the elders remained below at the foot of the mountain; and God gave him commandments. And Moses made known to the people the words of the Lord; and all the people answered with one voice and said, 'Everything that the Lord commands us we will do.'

Moses took blood with a hyssop, and sprinkled it upon the people, saying to them, 'This is the blood of the covenant,' and so forth. And God said to Moses, 'Say unto the children of Israel that they set apart for Me gold and silver and brass and purple,' and the rest of the things which are mentioned in the Tôrâh, 'and let them make a tabernacle for Me.' God also shewed the construction thereof to Moses, saying, 'Let Aaron and his sons be priests to Me, and let them serve My altar and sanctuary.'

God wrote ten commandments on two tables of stone, and these are they. Thou shalt not make to thyself an image or a likeness; thou shalt not falsify thy oaths; keep the day of the Sabbath; honour thy father and thy mother; thou shalt not do murder; thou shalt not commit adultery; thou shalt not steal; thou shalt not bear false witness; thou shalt not covet thy neighbour's or brother's house; thou shalt not covet the wife of thy kinsman or neighbour, nor his servants, nor his handmaidens. When the children of Israel saw that Moses tarried on the mountain, they gathered together to Aaron and said to him,

'Arise, make us a god to go before us, for we know not what has become of thy brother Moses.' Aaron said to them, 'Bring me the earrings that are in the ears of your wives and children.'

When they had brought them to him, he cast a calf from them, and said to the people, 'This is thy god, O Israel, who brought thee out of Egypt;' and they built an altar, and the children of Israel offered up sacrifice upon it. God said to Moses, 'Get thee down to the people, for they have become corrupt.' And Moses returned to the people, and in his hands were the two tablets of stone, upon which the ten commandments were written by the finger of God.

When Moses saw that the people had erred, he was angry and smote the tablets upon the side of the mountain and brake them. And Moses brought the calf, and filed it with a file, and threw it into the fire, and cast its ashes into water; and he commanded the children of Israel to drink of that water. And Moses reproached Aaron for his deeds, but Aaron said, 'Thou knowest that the people is stiffnecked.'

Then Moses said to the children of Levi, 'The Lord commands you that each man should slay his brother and his neighbour of those who have wrought iniquity;' and there were slain on that day three thousand men. And Moses went up to the mountain a second time, and there were with him two tables of stone instead of those which he brake. He remained on the mountain and fasted another forty days, praying and supplicating God to pardon the iniquity of the people.

When he came down from the mountain with the other two tablets upon which the commandments were written, the skin of his face shone, and the children of Israel were unable to look upon his countenance by reason of the radiance and light with which it was suffused; and they were afraid of him. When he came to the people, he covered his face with a napkin; and when he spake with God, he uncovered his face. And Moses said to Hur, the son of his father-in-law Reuel the Midianite, 'We will go to the land which God promised to give us; come with us, and we will do thee good;' but he would not, and returned to Midian. So the children of Israel went along the road to prepare a dwelling-place for themselves; and they lifted up their voice with a cry; and God heard and was angry, and fire went round about them and burnt up the parts round about their camps.

They said to Moses, 'Our soul languishes in this wilderness, and we remember the meats of Egypt; the fishes and the cucumbers and the melons and the onions and the leeks and the garlic; and now we have nought save this manna which is before us.' Now the appearance of manna was like that of coriander seed, and they ground it, and made flat cakes of it; and its taste was like bread with oil in it. And the Lord heard the voice of the people weeping each one at the door of his tent, and it was grievous to Him.

Moses prayed before the Lord and said, 'Why have I not found favour before Thee? and why hast Thou cast the weight of this people upon me? Did I beget them? Either slay me or let me find favour in Thy sight.' God said to Moses, 'Choose from the elders of the children of Israel seventy men, and gather them together to the tabernacle, and I will come down and speak with thee. And I will take of the spirit and power which is with thee and will lay it upon them, and they shall bear the burden of the people with thee, and thou shalt not bear it by thyself alone;' and Moses told them.

Moses gathered together seventy elders from the children of Israel, and the Lord came down in a cloud, and spake with them; and he took of the spirit and power which was with Moses and laid it upon them, and they prophesied. But two elders of the seventy whose names were written down remained in the camp and did not come; the name of the one was Eldad, and that of the other Medad; and they also prophesied in the tabernacle. A young man came and told Moses, and Joshua the son of Nun, the disciple of Moses, said to him, 'My lord, restrain them.' Moses said, 'Be not jealous; would that all the children of Israel were prophets; for the Spirit of God hath come upon them.'

And Moses said to the children of Israel, 'Because ye have wept and have asked for flesh, behold the Lord will give you flesh to eat; not one day, nor two, nor five, nor ten, but a month of days shall ye eat, until it goeth out of your nostrils, and becometh nauseous to you.' Moses said (to the Lord), 'This people among whom I am is six hundred thousand men, and hast Thou promised to feed them with flesh for a month of days? If we slay sheep and oxen, it would not suffice for them; and if we collect for them (all) the fish that are in the sea, they would not satisfy them.' And the Lord said to Moses, 'The hand of the Lord shall bring (this) to pass, and behold, thou shalt see whether this happens or not.' By the command of God a wind blew and brought out quails from the sea, and they were gathered around the camp of the children of Israel about a day's journey on all sides; and they were piled upon one another to the depth of two cubits. Each of the children of Israel gathered about ten cors; and they spread them out before the doors of their tents. And the Lord was angry with them, and smote them with death, and many died; and that place was called 'the graves of lust.'

They departed from thence to the place called Haserôth. And Aaron and Miriam lifted up themselves against Moses because of the Cushite woman whom he had married, and they said, 'Has God spoken with Moses only? Behold, He hath spoken with us also.' Now Moses was meeker than all men. And God heard the words of Miriam and Aaron, and came down in a pillar of cloud, and stood at the door of the tabernacle, and called them, and they came forth to Him. The Lord said to them, 'Hear what I will say to you. I have revealed Myself to you in secret, and ye have prophesied in a dream. Not so with My servant Moses, who is trusted in everything, for with him I speak mouth to mouth.' And the Lord was angry with them, and the cloud was taken up from the tabernacle; and Miriam was a leper, and was white as snow. Aaron saw that she was a leper, and said to Moses, 'I entreat thee not to look upon our sins which we have sinned against thee.' Moses made supplication before God, saying, 'Heal her, O Lord, I entreat Thee.' God said to Moses, 'If her father had spat in her face, it would have been right for her to pass the night alone outside the camp for seven days, and then to come in.' So Miriam stayed outside the camp for seven days, and then she was purified.

And God said to Moses, 'Send forth spies, from every tribe a man, and let them go and search out the land of promise.' Moses chose twelve men, among whom were Joshua the son of Nun and Caleb the son of Jephunneh; and they went and searched out the land. And they returned, carrying with them of the fruit of the land grapes and figs and pomegranates. The spies came and said, 'We have not strength to stand against them, for they are mighty men, while we are like miserable locusts in their sight.' And the children of Israel were gathered together to Moses and Aaron, and they lifted up their voice and wept with a great weeping, saying, 'Why did we not die under the hand of the Lord in the wilderness and in Egypt, and not come to this land to die with our wives and children, and to become a laughing-stock and a scorn to the nations?'

Joshua the son of Nun and Caleb the son of Jephunneh said to them, 'Fear not; we will go up against them, and the Lord will deliver them into our hands, and we shall inherit the land, as the Lord said to us.' The children of Israel said to one another, 'Come, let us make us a chief and return to Egypt;' and Moses and Aaron fell upon their faces before the people. And Joshua the son of Nun and Caleb the son of Jephunneh rent their clothes and said to the children of Israel, 'The land which we have searched out is a thriving one, flowing with milk and honey, and it is in the power of God to give it to us; do not provoke God.'

And the children of Israel gathered together to stone them with stones. And God was revealed in a cloud over the tabernacle openly in the sight of the children of Israel; and He said to Moses, 'How long will these (people) provoke Me? and how long will they not believe in Me for all the wonders which I have wrought among them? Let Me smite them, and I will make thee the chief of a people stronger than they.'

Moses said to the Lord, 'O Lord God Almighty, the Egyptians will hear and will say that Thou hast brought out Thy people from among them by Thy power: but when Thou smitest them, they will say, "He slew them in the desert, because He was unable to make them inherit the land which He promised them."

And Thou, O Lord, who hast dwelt among this people, and they have seen Thee eye to eye, and Thy light is ever abiding with them, and Thou goest (before them) by night in a pillar of light, and dost shade them with a cloud by day, pardon now in Thy mercy the sins of Thy people, as Thou hast pardoned their sins from Egypt unto here.'

The Sealed Magical Book of Moses

God said to Moses, 'Say unto the children of Israel, O wicked nation, I have heard all the words which ye have spoken, and I will do unto you even as ye wish for yourselves. In this desert shall your dead bodies fall, and your families and your children, every one that knows good from evil, from twenty years old and downwards. Their children shall enter the land of promise; but ye shall not enter it, save Caleb the son of Jephunneh and Joshua the son of Nun. Your children shall remain in this wilderness forty years, until your dead bodies decay, according to the number of the days in which ye searched out the land; for each day ye shall be requited with a year because of your sins.'

And the spies who had spied out the land with Joshua the son of Nun and Caleb the son of Jephunneh died at once, save Joshua the son of Nun and Caleb the son of Jephunneh. This was very grievous to the people, and the children of Israel said to Moses, 'Behold, we are going up to the land which God promised us.'

He said to them, 'God hath turned His face from you; go ye not away from your place.' And they hearkened not to Moses, but went up to the top of the mountain without Moses and the tabernacle; and the Amalekites and Canaanites who dwelt there came out against them and put them to flight. God said to Moses, 'When the children of Israel enter the land of promise, let them offer as offerings fine flour and oil and wine.' Then Korah the son of Zahar (Izhar), and Dathan and Abiram the sons of Eliab, together with their families, and two hundred and fifty men, separated from the children of Israel; and they came to Moses, and made him hear them, and troubled him.

And Moses fell upon his face before the Lord and said, 'Tomorrow shall every one know whom God chooses. Is that which I have done for you not sufficient for you, that ye serve before the Lord, but ye must seek the priesthood also?'

And Moses said unto God, 'O God, receive not their offerings.' And Moses said to them, 'Let every one of you take his censer in his hand, and place fire and incense therein;' and there stood before the Lord on that day two hundred and fifty men holding their censers. The Lord said to Moses, 'Stand aloof from the people, and I will destroy them in a moment.' And Moses and Aaron fell upon their faces, and said to the Lord, 'Wilt Thou destroy all these for the sake of one man who hath sinned?'

God said to Moses, 'Tell the children of Israel to go away from around the tents of Korah and his fellows;' and Moses said to the people everything that God had said to him; and the people kept away from the tent of Korah. Then Korah and his family with their wives and children came forth and stood at the doors of their tents. And Moses said to them, 'If God hath sent me, let the earth open her mouth and swallow them up; but if I am come of my own desire, let them die a natural death like every man.' While the word was yet in his mouth, the earth opened, and swallowed them up, and the people that were with them, from man even unto beast; and fear fell upon their companions. The fire went forth from their censers, and burnt up the two hundred and fifty men. Moses said to Eleazar, 'Take their censers and make a casting of them, that they may be a memorial, for they have been sanctified by the fire which fell into them, that no man who is not of the family of Aaron should dare to take a censer in his hand.'

The children of Israel gathered together unto Moses and Aaron and said to them, 'Ye have destroyed the people of the Lord.' And God said to Moses and Aaron in the tabernacle, 'Stand aloof from them, and I will destroy them in a moment.' Moses said to Aaron, 'Take a censer and put fire and incense therein, and go to the people, that God may forgive their sins, for anger has gone forth against them from before the Lord.' And Aaron put incense in a censer, and went to the people in haste, and he saw death destroying the people unsparingly; but with his censer he separated the living from the dead, and the plague was stayed from them. The number of men whom the plague destroyed at that time of the children of Israel was fourteen thousand and seven hundred, besides those who died with the children of Korah; and Aaron returned to Moses. And God said to Moses, 'Let the children of Israel collect from every tribe a rod, and let them write the name of the tribe upon its rod, and the name of Aaron upon (that of) the tribe of Levi, and the rod of the man whom the Lord chooseth shall blossom.' And they did as God had commanded them, and took the rods and placed them in the tabernacle that day. On the morrow Moses went into the tabernacle, and saw the rod of the house of Levi budding and bearing almonds. And Moses brought out all the rods to the children of Israel, and the sons of Levi were set apart for the service of the priesthood before the Lord.

When the children of Israel came to the wilderness of Sîn, Miriam the sister of Moses and Aaron died, and they buried her. And there was no water for them to drink; and the children of Israel murmured against Moses and said, 'Would that we had all died with those who are dead already, and that we had not come hither to die with our beasts and our possessions! Why did the Lord bring us out from Egypt to this desert land, in which there are neither pomegranates nor grapes?' Moses and Aaron went to the tabernacle, and fell upon their faces before the Lord, and the Lord said to them, 'Gather together the children of Israel, and let Moses smite the rock with the rod, and water shall come forth and all the people shall drink;' and Moses called that water 'the water of strife.' The children of Israel gathered themselves together unto Moses and Aaron, and they murmured against them saying, 'Why have ye brought us out to this desert to die of thirst and hunger?' And the Lord was angry with them, and sent serpents upon them, and many of the people died by reason of the serpents. And they gathered themselves together unto Moses and Aaron and said to them, 'We have sinned before God and before you.' God said to Moses, 'Make a serpent of brass, and hang it upon the top of thy rod, and set it up among the people; and let every one whom a serpent shall bite look upon the brazen serpent, and he shall live and not die.' This serpent which Moses set up is a type of the crucifixion of our Lord, as the doctor saith, 'Like the serpent which Moses set up, He set Him up also, that He might heal men of the bites of cruel demons.'

And the children of Israel came to mount Hôr, and Aaron died there; and they wept for him a month of days; and Moses put his garments upon Eleazar his son. The children of Israel began to commit fornication with the daughters of Moab, and to bow down to their idols, and to eat of their sacrifices. The Lord was angry with them, and He commanded Moses to gather together the children of Israel, and to order every man to slay his fellow, and every one who should bow down to Baal Peôr, the idol of the Moabites. When they were all assembled at the door of the tabernacle, Zimri the son of Salô came and took

Cosbî the daughter of Zûr, and committed fornication with her in the sight of Moses and all the people; and God smote the people with a pestilence. Then Phinehas the son of Eleazar the priest, the son of Aaron, arose, and thrust them through with a spear, and lifted them up upon the top of it; and the plague was stayed from that hour. This zeal was accounted unto Phinehas as a prayer; as the blessed David says1, 'Phinehas arose and prayed, and the pestilence was stayed; and it was accounted unto him for merit from generation unto generation, even for ever.' The number of those who died at that time was twenty-four thousand men. God commanded Moses to number the people, and their number amounted to six hundred and one thousand seven hundred and eighty souls.

And God commanded Moses to bless Joshua the son of Nun, and to lay his hand upon him, and to set him up before Eleazar the priest and before all the children of Israel; and God gave him wisdom and knowledge and prophecy and courage, and made him ruler of the children of Israel. God commanded the children of Israel to destroy the Midianites. And (Moses) chose from each tribe a thousand men, and they went up against the Midianites and took them captive and spoiled them. And Moses told them to slay every man who had committed fornication with a Midianitish woman, and every Midianitish woman who had committed fornication with a son of Israel, except the virgins whom man had not known. God commanded Moses to set apart one-fiftieth part of the spoil for the sons of Levi, the ministers of the altar and the house of the Lord. The number of the flocks that were gathered together with the children of Israel was six hundred and seventy thousand, and seventy-two thousand oxen, and thirty-two thousand virgins.

And the Lord commanded them that when they should pass over the Jordan and come to the land of promise, they should set apart three villages for a place of flight and refuge, that whosoever committed a murder involuntarily might flee thither and dwell in them until the high priest of that time died, when he might return to his family and the house of his fathers. God laid down for them laws and commandments, and these are they. A man shall not clothe himself in a woman's garments, neither shall a woman clothe herself in those of a man. If one sees a bird's nest, he shall drive away the mother, and then take the young ones. A man shall make a fence and an enclosure to his roof, lest any one fall therefrom, and his blood be required of him. Let him that hath a rebellious son, bring him out before the elders, and let them reprimand him; if he turn from his (evil) habit, (goad and well); but if not, let him be stoned. One that is crucified shall not pass the night upon his cross5. He that blasphemes God shall be slain. The man that lies with a betrothed woman shall be slain. If she is not betrothed, he shall give her father five hundred dinârs, and take her to wife. And the other commandments.

And Moses gathered together the children of Israel and said to them, 'Behold, I am a hundred and twenty years old, no more strength abideth in me; and God hath said to me, Thou shalt not pass over this river Jordan.' And he called Joshua the son of Nun and said to him in the sight of all the people, 'Be strong and of good courage, for thou shalt bring this people into the land of promise. Fear not the nations that are in it, for God will deliver them into thy hands, and thou shalt inherit their cities and villages, and shalt destroy them.'

And Moses wrote down laws and judgements and orders, and gave them into the hands of the priests, the children of Levi. He commanded them that, when they crossed over to the land of promise, they should make a feast of tabernacles and should read aloud these commandments before all the people, men and women; that they might hear and fear the Lord their God.

And God said to Moses, 'Behold thou art going the way of thy fathers; call Joshua the son of Nun, thy disciple, and make him stand in the tabernacle, and command him to be diligent for the government of this people; for I know that after thy death they will turn aside from the way of truth, and will worship idols, and I will turn away My face from them.' And God said to Moses, 'Get thee up into this mountain of the Amorites which is called Nebo, and see the land of Canaan, and be gathered to thy fathers, even as Aaron thy brother died on mount Hôr.'

So Moses died there and was buried, and no man knoweth his grave; for God hid him, that the children of Israel might not go astray and worship him as God. He died at the age of one hundred and twenty years; his sight had not diminished, neither was the complexion of his face changed. And the children of Israel wept for him a month of days in Arbôth Moab. From Adam then until the death of Moses was three thousand eight hundred and sixty-eight years.

When the number of the children of Israel was reckoned up, it amounted to eight hundred thousand, and that of the house of Judah to five hundred thousand. In the Book of Chronicles it is written, 'The children of Israel were a thousand thousand, one hundred thousand and one hundred men; and the house of Judah was four hundred thousand and seven hundred men that drew sword.' Now when they came out of Egypt, they were six hundred thousand; and when they entered Egypt, they were seventy and five souls.

THE TRANSFIGURATION OF MOSES

I saw that the faith of the disciples was greatly strengthened at the transfiguration. God chose to give the followers of Jesus strong proof that he was the promised Messiah, that in their bitter sorrow and disappointment they should not entirely cast away their confidence. At the transfiguration the Lord sent Moses and Elias to talk with Jesus concerning his suffering and death. Instead of choosing angels to converse with his Son, God chose those who had an experience in the trials of earth. A few of his followers were permitted to be with him and behold his face lighted up with divine glory, and witness his raiment white and glistening, and hear the voice of God, in fearful majesty, saying, This is my beloved Son, hear him.

Elijah had walked with God. His work had not been pleasant. God, through him, had reproved sin. He was a prophet of God, and had to flee from place to place to save his life. He was hunted like the wild beasts that they might destroy him. God translated Elijah. Angels bore him in glory and triumph to heaven.

Moses had been a man greatly honored of God. He was greater than any who had lived before him. He was privileged to talk with God face to face as a man speaketh with a friend. He was permitted to see the bright light and excellent glory that enshrouded the Father. Through Moses the Lord delivered the children of Israel from Egyptian bondage. Moses was a mediator for the children of Israel. He often stood between them and the wrath of God. When the wrath of God was greatly kindled against Israel for their unbelief, their murmurings, and their grievous sins, Moses' love for them was tested. God promised him that if he would let Israel go, let them be destroyed, he would make of him a mighty nation. Moses showed his love for Israel by his earnest pleading. In his distress he prayed God to turn from his fierce anger, and forgive Israel, or blot his name out of his book.

When Israel murmured against God and against Moses, because they could get no water, they accused him of leading them out to kill them and their children. God heard their murmurings, and bade Moses smite the rock, that the children of Israel might have water. Moses smote the rock in wrath, and took the glory to himself. The continual waywardness and murmuring of the children of Israel had caused him the keenest sorrow, and for a little he forgot how much God had borne with them, and that their murmuring was not against Moses, but against God. He thought only of himself, how deeply he was wronged, and how little gratitude they manifested in return, for his deep love for them.

As Moses smote the rock, he failed to honor God, and magnify him before the children of Israel, that they might glorify God. And the Lord was displeased with Moses, and said that he should not enter the promised land. It was God's plan to often prove Israel by bringing them into strait places, and then in their great necessity exhibit his power, that he might live in their memory, and they glorify him.

When Moses came down from the mount with the two tables of stone, and saw Israel worshiping the golden calf, his anger was greatly kindled, and he threw down the tables of stone, and broke them. I saw that Moses did not sin in this. He was wroth for God, jealous for his glory. But when he yielded to the natural feelings of the heart, and took glory to himself, which was due to God, he sinned, and for that sin, God would not suffer him to enter the promised land.

The Sealed Magical Book of Moses

Satan had been trying to find something wherewith to accuse Moses before the angels. Satan triumphed in that he had caused him to displease God, and he exulted, and told the angels that when the Saviour of the world should come to redeem man, he could overcome him. For this transgression Moses came under the power of Satan - the dominion of death. Had he remained steadfast, and not sinned in taking glory to himself, the Lord would have brought him to the promised land, and then translated him to heaven without seeing death.

I saw that Moses passed through death, but Michael came down and gave him life before he saw corruption. Satan claimed the body as his, but Michael resurrected Moses, and took him to heaven. The Devil tried to hold his body, and railed out bitterly against God, denounced him as unjust, in taking from him his prey. But Michael did not rebuke the Devil, although it was through his temptation and power that God's servant had fallen. Christ meekly referred him to his Father, saying, The Lord rebuke thee.

Jesus told his disciples that there were some standing with him who should not taste of death till they should see the kingdom of God come with power. At the transfiguration this promise was fulfilled. The fashion of Jesus' countenance was changed, and shone like the sun. His raiment was white and glistening. Moses was present, and represented those who will be raised from the dead at the second appearing of Jesus. And Elias, who was translated without seeing death, represented those who will be changed to immortality at Christ's second coming, and without seeing death will be translated to heaven. The disciples beheld with fear and astonishment the excellent majesty of Jesus, and the cloud that overshadowed them, and heard the voice of God in terrible majesty, saying, This is my beloved Son, hear him.

See Exodus chap. 32; Numbers 20:7-12; Deuteronomy 34:5; 2 Kings 2:11; Mark chap. 9; Jude 9

MOSES AND THE TABERNACLE IN THE WILDERNESS

There is no doubt that much of the material recorded in the first five books of the Old Testament is derived from the initiatory rituals of the Egyptian Mysteries. The priests of Isis were deeply versed in occult lore, and the Israelites during their captivity in Egypt learned from them many things concerning the significance of Divinity and the manner of worshiping It. The authorship of the first five books of the Old Testament is generally attributed to Moses, but whether or not he was the actual writer of them is a matter of controversy. There is considerable evidence to substantiate the hypothesis that the Pentateuch was compiled at a much later date, from oral traditions. Concerning the authorship of these books, Thomas Inman makes a rather startling statement: "It is true that we have books which purport to be the books of Moses; so there are, or have been, books purporting to be written by Homer, Orpheus, Enoch, Mormon, and Junius; yet the existence of the writings, and the belief that they were written by those whose name they bear, are no real evidences of the men or the genuineness of the works called by their names. It is true also that Moses is spoken of occasionally in the time of the early Kings of Jerusalem; but it is clear that these passages are written by a late hand, and have been introduced into the places where they are found, with the definite intention of making it appear that the lawgiver was known to David and Solomon."

While this noted scholar undoubtedly had much evidence to support his belief, it seems that this statement is somewhat too sweeping in character. It is apparently based upon the fact that Thomas Inman doubted the historical existence of Moses. This doubt was based upon the etymological resemblance of the word Moses to an ancient name for the sun. As the result of these deductions, Inman sought to prove that the Lawgiver of Israel was merely another form of the omnipresent solar myth. While Inman demonstrated that by transposing two of the ancient letters the word Moses (השמ) became Shemmah (המש), an appellation of the celestial globe, he seems to have overlooked the fact that in the ancient Mysteries the initiates were often given names synonymous with the sun, to symbolize the fact that the redemption and regeneration of the solar power had been achieved within their own natures. It is far more probable that the man whom we know as Moses was an accredited representative of the secret schools, laboring, as many other emissaries have labored, to instruct primitive races in the mysteries of their immortal souls.

The true name of the Grand Old Man of Israel who is known to history as Moses will probably never be ascertained. The word Moses, when understood in its esoteric Egyptian sense, means one who has been admitted into the Mystery Schools of Wisdom and as gone forth to teach the ignorant concerning the will of the gods and the mysteries of life, as these mysteries were explained within the temples of Isis, Osiris, and Serapis. There is much controversy concerning the nationality of Moses. Some assert that he was a Jew, adopted and educated by the ruling house of Egypt; others hold the opinion that he was a full-blooded Egyptian. A few even believe him to be identical with the immortal Hermes, for both these illustrious founders of religious systems received tablets from heaven supposedly written by the finger of God. The stories told concerning Moses, his discovery in the ark of bulrushes by Pharaoh's daughter, his adoption into the royal family of Egypt, and his later revolt against Egyptian autocracy coincide exactly with certain ceremonies through which the candidates of the Egyptian Mysteries passed in their ritualistic wanderings in search of truth and understanding. The analogy can also be traced in the movements of the heavenly bodies.

It is not strange that the erudite Moses, initiated in Egypt, should teach the Jews a philosophy containing the more important principles of Egyptian esotericism. The religions of Egypt at the time of the Israelitic captivity were far older than even the Egyptians themselves realized. Histories were difficult to compile in those days, and the Egyptians were satisfied to trace their race back to a mythological period when the gods themselves walked the earth and with their own power established the Double Empire of the Nile. The Egyptians did not dream that these divine progenitors were the Atlanteans, who, forced to abandon their seven islands because of volcanic cataclysms, had immigrated into Egypt--then an Atlantean colony--where they established a great philosophic and literary center of civilization which was later to influence profoundly the religions and science of unnumbered races and peoples. Today

The Sealed Magical Book of Moses

Egypt is forgotten, but things Egyptian will always be remembered and revered. Egypt is dead, yet it lives immortal in its philosophy, and architectonics.

As Odin founded his Mysteries in Scandinavia, and Quexalcoatl in Mexico, so Moses, laboring with the then nomadic people of Israel's twelve tribes, established in the midst of them his secret and symbolic school, which has came to be known as The Tabernacle Mysteries. The Tabernacle of: the Jews was merely a temple patterned after the temples of Egypt, and transportable to meet the needs of that roving disposition which the Israelites were famous. Every part of the Tabernacle and the enclosure which surrounded it was symbolic of some great natural or philosophic truth. To the ignorant it was but a place to which to bring offerings and in which to make sacrifice; to the wise it was a temple of learning, sacred to the Universal Spirit of Wisdom.

While the greatest, minds of the Jewish and Christian worlds have realized that the Bible is a book of allegories, few seem to have taken the trouble to investigate its symbols and parables. When Moses instituted his Mysteries, he is said to have given to a chosen few initiates certain oral teachings which could never be written but were to be preserved from one generation to the next by word-of-mouth transmission. Those instructions were in the form of philosophical keys, by means of which the allegories were made to reveal their hidden significance. These mystic keys to their sacred writings were called by the Jews the Qabbalah (Cabala, Kaballah).

The modern world seems to have forgotten the existence of those unwritten teachings which explained satisfactorily the apparent contradictions of the written Scriptures, nor does it remember that the pagans appointed their two-faced Janus as custodian of the key to the Temple of Wisdom. Janus has been metamorphosed into St. Peter, so often symbolized as holding in his hand the key to the gate of heaven. The gold and silver keys of "God's Vicar on Earth," the Pope, symbolizes this "secret doctrine" which, when properly understood, unlocks the treasure chest of the Christian and Jewish Qabbalah.

The temples of Egyptian mysticism (from which the Tabernacle was copied) were, according to their own priests, miniature representations of the universe.

The solar system was always regarded as a great temple of initiation, which candidates entered through the gates of birth; after threading the tortuous passageways of earthly existence, they finally approached the veil of the Great Mystery--Death--through whose gate they vanished back into the invisible world. Socrates subtly reminded his disciples that Death was, in reality, the great initiation, for his last words were: "Crito, I owe a cock to Asclepius; will you remember to pay the debt?" (As the rooster was sacred to the gods and the sacrifice of this bird accompanied a candidate's introduction into the Mysteries, Socrates implied that he was about to take his great initiation.)

Life is the great mystery, and only those who pass successfully through its tests and trials, interpreting them aright and extracting the essence of experience therefrom, achieve true understanding. Thus, the temples were built in the form of the world and their rituals were based upon life and its multitudinous problems. Nor only was the Tabernacle itself patterned according to Egyptian mysticism; its utensils were also of ancient and accepted form. The Ark of the Covenant itself was an adaptation of the Egyptian Ark, even to the kneeling figures upon its lid. Bas-reliefs on the Temple of Philæ show Egyptian priests carrying their Ark, which closely resembled the Ark of the Jews, upon their shoulders by means of staves like those described in Exodus.

The following description of the Tabernacle and its priests is based upon the account of its construction and ceremonies recorded by Josephus in the Third Book of his Antiquities of the Jews. The Bible references are from a "Breeches" Bible (famous for its rendering of the seventh verse of the third chapter of Genesis), printed in London in 1599, and the quotations are reproduced in their original spelling and punctuation.

THE BUILDING OF THE TABERNACLE

Moses, speaking for Jehovah, the God of Israel, appointed two architects to superintend the building of the Tabernacle. They were Besaleel, the son of Uri, of the tribe of Judah, and Aholiab, the son of Ahisamach, of the tribe of Dan. Their popularity was so great that they were also the unanimous choice of the people. When Jacob upon his deathbed blessed his sons (see Genesis xlix), he assigned to each a symbol. The symbol of Judah was a lion; that of Dan a serpent or a bird (possibly an eagle). The lion and the eagle are two of the four beasts of the Cherubim (the fixed signs of the zodiac); and the Rosicrucian alchemists maintained that the mysterious Stone of the Wise (the Soul) was compounded with the aid of the Blood of the Red Lion and the Gluten of the White Eagle. It seems probable that there is a hidden mystic relationship between fire (the Red Lion), water (the White Eagle), as they were used in occult chemistry, and the representatives of these two tribes whose symbols were identical with these alchemical elements.

As the Tabernacle was the dwelling place of God among men, likewise the soul body in man is the dwelling place of his divine nature, round which gathers a twelvefold material constitution in the same manner that the tribes of Israel camped about the enclosure sacred to Jehovah. The idea that the Tabernacle was really symbolic of an invisible spiritual truth outside the comprehension of the Israelites is substantiated by a statement made in the eighth chapter of Hebrews: "Who serve unto the paterne and shadowe of heavenly things, as Moses was warned by God, when he was about to finish the Tabernacle." Here we find the material physical place of worship called a "shadow" or symbol of a spiritual institution, invisible but omnipotent.

The specifications of the Tabernacle are described in the book of Exodus, twenty-fifth chapter: "Then the Lord spake unto Moses, saying, Speake unto the children of Israel that they receive an offering for me: of every man, whose heart giveth it freely, yee shall take the offering for me. And this is the offering which ye shall take of them, gold and silver, and brass, and blue silke, and purple, and scarlet, and fine linnen and goats haire. And rammes skinnes coloured red, and the skinnes of badgers, and the wood Shittim, oyle for the light, spices for anoynting oyle, and for the perfume of sweet favour, onix stones, and stories to be set in the Ephod, and in the breastplate. Also they shall make me a Sanctuary, that I may dwell among them. According to all that I shew thee, even so shall ye make the forme of the Tabernacle, and the fashion of all the instruments thereof."

The Sealed Magical Book of Moses

The court of the Tabernacle was an enclosed area, fifty cubits wide and one hundred cubits long, circumscribed by a wall of linen curtains hung from brazen pillars five cubits apart. (The cubit is an ancient standard of measurement, its length being equal to the distance between the elbow and the extreme end of the index finger, approximately eighteen inches.) There were twenty of these pillars on each of the longer sides and ten on the shorter. Each pillar had a base of brass and a capital of silver. The Tabernacle was always laid out with the long sides facing north and south and the short sides facing east and west, with the entrance to the east, thus showing the influence of primitive sun worship.

The outer court served the principal purpose of isolating the tent of the Tabernacle proper, which stood in the midst of the enclosure. At the entrance to the courtyard, which was in the eastern face of the rectangle, stood the Altar of Burnt Offerings, made of brass plates over wood and ornamented with the horns of bulls and rams. Farther in, but on a line with this altar, stood the Laver of Purification, a great vessel containing water for priestly ablutions. The Laver was twofold in its construction, the upper part being a large bowl, probably covered, which served as a source of supply for a lower basin in which the priests bathed themselves before participating in the various ceremonials. It is supposed that this Laver was encrusted with the metal mirrors of the women of the twelve tribes of Israel.

The dimensions of the Tabernacle proper were as follows: "Its length, when it was set up, was thirty cubits, and its breadth was ten cubits. The one of its walls was on the south, and the other was exposed to the north, and on the back part of it remained the west. It was necessary that its height should be equal to its breadth (ten cubits)." (Josephus.)

It is the custom of bibliologists to divide the interior of the Tabernacle into two rooms: one room ten cubits wide, ten cubits high, and twenty cubits long, which was called the Holy Place and contained three special articles of furniture, namely, the Seven-Branched Candlestick, the Table of the Shewbread, and the Altar of Burnt Incense; the other room ten cubits wide, ten cubits high, and ten cubits long, which was called the Holy of Holies and contained but one article of furniture—the Ark of the Covenant. The two rooms were separated from each other by an ornamental veil upon which were embroidered many kinds of flowers, but no animal or human figures.

Josephus hints that there was a third compartment which was formed by subdividing the Holy Place, at least hypothetically, into two chambers. The Jewish historian is not very explicit in his description of this third room, and the majority of writers seem to have entirely overlooked and neglected this point, although Josephus emphatically states that Moses himself divided the inner tent into three sections. The veil separating the Holy Place from the Holy of Holies was hung across four pillars, which probably indicated in a subtle way the four elements, while at the entrance to the tent proper the Jews placed seven pillars, referring to the seven senses and the seven vowels of the Sacred Name. That later only five pillars are mentioned may be accounted for by the fact that at the present time man has only five developed senses and five active vowels. The early Jewish writer of The Baraitha treats of the curtains as follows:

"There were provided ten curtains of blue, of purple, and scarlet, and fine-twined linen. As is said, 'Moreover thou shall make the tabernacle with ten curtains of fine-twined linen, and blue, and purple, and scarlet.' There were provided eleven curtains of goats' hair, and the length of every one of them was thirty cubits. Rabbi Judah said, 'There were two covers-the lower one of rams' skins dyed red, and the upper one of badgers' skins. '"

Calmet is of the opinion that the Hebrew word translated "badger" really means "dark purple" and therefore did not refer to any particular animal, but probably to a heavily woven waterproof fabric of dark and inconspicuous color. During the time of Israel's wanderings through the wilderness, it is supposed that a pillar of fire hovered over the Tabernacle at night, while a column of smoke traveled with it by day. This cloud was called by the Jews the Shechinah and was symbolic of the presence of the Lord. In one of the early Jewish books rejected at the time of the compiling of the Talmud the following description of the Shechinah appears:

"Then a cloud covered the tent of the congregation, and the glory of the Lord filled the Tabernacle. And that was one of the clouds of glory, which served the

Israelites in the wilderness forty years. One on the right hand, and one on the left, and one before them, and one behind them. And one over them, and a cloud dwelling in their midst (and the cloud, the Shechinah which was in the tent), and the pillar of cloud which moved before them, making low before them the high places, and making high before them the low places, and killing serpents and scorpions, and burning thorns and briars, and guiding them in the straight way." (From The Baraitha, the Book of the Tabernacle.)

THE FURNISHINGS OF THE TABERNACLE

There is no doubt that the Tabernacle, its furnishings and ceremonials, when considered esoterically, are analogous to the structure, organs, and functions of the human body. At the entrance to the outer court of the Tabernacle stood the Altar of Burnt Offerings, five cubits long and five cubits wide but only three cubits high. Its upper surface was a brazen grill upon which the sacrifice was placed, while beneath was a space for the fire. This altar signified that a candidate, when first entering the precincts of sanctuary, must offer upon the brazen altar not a poor unoffending bull or ram but its correspondence within his own nature. The bull, being symbolic of earthiness, represented his own gross constitution which must be burned up by the fire of his Divinity. (The sacrificing of beasts, and in some cases human beings, upon the altars of the pagans was the result of their ignorance concerning the fundamental principle underlying sacrifice. They did not realize that their offerings must come from within their own natures in order to be acceptable.)

Farther westward, in line with the Brazen Altar, was the Laver of Purification already described. It signified to the priest that he should cleanse not only his body but also his soul from all stains of impurity, for none who is not clean in both body and mind can enter into the presence of Divinity and live. Beyond the Laver of Purification was the entrance to the Tabernacle proper, facing the east, so that the first rays of the rising sun might enter and light the chamber. Between the encrusted pillars could be seen the Holy Place, a mysterious chamber, its walls hung with magnificent drapes embroidered with the faces of Cherubs.

The Sealed Magical Book of Moses

Against the wall on the southern side of the Holy Place stood the great Candlestick, or lampstand, of cast gold, which was believed to weigh about a hundred pounds. From its central shaft branched out six arms, each ending in a cup-shaped depression in which stood an oil lamp. There were seven lamps, three on the arms at each side and one on the central stem. The Candlestick was ornamented with seventy-two almonds, knops, and flowers. Josephus says seventy, but wherever this round number is used by the Hebrews it really means seventy-two. Opposite the Candlestick, against the northern wall, was a table bearing twelve loaves of Shewbread in two stacks of six loaves each. (Calmet is of the opinion that the bread was not stacked up but spread out on the table in two rows, each containing six loaves.) On this table also stood two lighted incensories, which were placed upon the tops of the stacks of Shewbread so that the smoke of the incense might be an acceptable aroma to the Lord, bearing with it in its ascent the soul of the Shewbread.

In the center of the room, almost against the partition leading into the Holy of Holies, stood the Altar of Burnt Incense, made of wood overlaid with golden plates. Its width and length were each a cubit and its height was two cubits. This altar was symbolic of the human larynx, from which the words of man's mouth ascend as an acceptable offering unto the Lord, for the larynx occupies the position in the constitution of man between the Holy Place, which is the trunk of his body, and the Holy of Holies, which is the head with its contents.

Into the Holy of Holies none might pass save the High Priest, and he only at certain prescribed times, The room contained no furnishings save the Ark of the Covenant, which stood against the western wall, opposite the entrance. In Exodus the dimensions of the Ark are given as two and a half cubits for its length, one cubit and a half its breadth and one cubit and a half its height. It was made of shittim-wood, gold plated within and without, and contained the sacred tablets of the Law delivered to Moses upon Sinai. The lid of the Ark was in the form of a golden plate upon which knelt two mysterious creatures called Cherubim, facing each other, with wings arched overhead. It was upon this mercy seat between the wings of the celestials that the Lord of Israel descended when He desired to communicate with His High Priest.

The Sealed Magical Book of Moses

The furnishings of the Tabernacle were made conveniently portable. Each altar and implement of any size was supplied with staves which could be put: through rings; by this means it could be picked up and carried by four or more bearers. The staves were never removed from the Ark of the Covenant until it was finally placed in the Holy of Holies of the Everlasting House, King Solomon's Temple.

There is no doubt that the Jews in early times realized, at least in part, that their Tabernacle was a symbolic edifice. Josephus realized this and while he has been severely criticized because he interpreted the Tabernacle symbolism according to Egyptian and Grecian paganism, his description of the secret meanings of its drapes and furnishings is well worthy of consideration. He says:

"When Moses distinguished the tabernacle into three parts, and allowed two of them to the priests, as a place accessible and common, he denoted the land and the sea, these being of general access to all; but he set apart the third division for God, because heaven is inaccessible to men. And when he ordered twelve loaves to be set on a table, he denoted the year, as distinguished into so many months. By branching out the candlestick into seventy parts, he secretly intimated the Decani, or seventy divisions of the planets; and as to the seven lamps upon the candlesticks, they referred to the course of the planets, of which that is the number. The veils too, which were composed of four things, they declared the four elements; for the plain linen was proper to signify the earth, because the flax grows out of the earth; the purple signified the sea, because that color is dyed by the blood of a sea shell-fish; the blue is fit to signify the air; and the scarlet will naturally be an indication of fire.

"Now the vestment of the high-priest being made of linen, signified the earth; the blue denoted the sky, being like lightning in its pomegranates, and in the noise of the bells resembling thunder. And for the Ephod, it showed that God had made the universe of four (elements); and as for the gold interwoven, it related to the splendor by which all things are enlightened. He also appointed the breastplate to be placed in the middle of the Ephod, to resemble the earth, for that has the very middle place of the world. And the girdle which encompassed the high-priest round signified the ocean, for that goes round about and includes the universe. Each of the sardonyxes declares to us the sun and the moon, those, I mean, that were in the nature of buttons on the high-priest's shoulders. And for the twelve stones, whether we understand by them the months, or whether we understand the like number of the signs of that circle which the Greeks call the Zodiac, we shall not be mistaken in their meaning. And for the mitre, which was of a blue colour, it seems to me to mean heaven; for how otherwise could the name of God be inscribed upon it? That it was also illustrated with a crown, and that of gold also, is because of that splendour with which God is pleased." It is also symbolically significant that the Tabernacle was built in seven months and dedicated to God at the time of the new moon.

The metals used in the building of the Tabernacle were all emblematic. Gold represents spirituality, and the golden plates laid over the shittim-wood were emblems of the spiritual nature which glorifies the human nature symbolized by the wood. Mystics have taught that man's physical body is surrounded by a series of invisible bodies of diverse colors and great splendor. In the majority of people the spiritual nature is concealed and imprisoned in the material nature, but in a few this internal constitution has been objectified and the spiritual nature is outside, so that it surrounds man's personality with a great radiance.

Silver, used as the capitals for the pillars, has its reference to the moon, which was sacred to the Jews and the Egyptians alike. The priests held secret ritualistic ceremonies at the time of the new and the full moon, both of which periods were sacred to Jehovah. Silver, so the ancients taught, was gold with its sun-ray turned inward instead of objectified. While gold symbolized the spiritual soul, silver represented the purified and regenerated human nature of man.

The brass used in the outer altars was a composite substance consisting of an alloy of precious and base metals. Thus, it represented the constitution of the average individual, who is a combination of both the higher and the lower elements.

The three divisions of the Tabernacle should have a special interest to Freemasons, for they represent the three degrees of the Blue Lodge, while the three orders of priests who served the Tabernacle are preserved to modern Masonry as the Entered Apprentice, the Fellow Craftsman, and the Master Mason. The Hawaiian Islanders built a Tabernacle not unlike that of the Jews, except that their rooms were one above another and not one behind another, as in the case of the Tabernacle of the Israelites. The three rooms are also the three important chambers of the Great Pyramid of Gizeh.

THE ROBES OF GLORY

As explained in the quotation from Josephus, the robes and adornments of the Jewish priests had a secret significance, and even to this day there is a religious cipher language concealed in the colors, forms, and uses of sacred garments, not only among the Christian and Jewish priests but also among pagan religions. The vestments of the Tabernacle priests were called Cahanææ; those of the High Priest were termed Cahanææ Rabbæ. Over the Machanese, an undergarment resembling short trousers, they wore the Chethone, a finely woven linen robe, which reached to the ground and had long sleeves tied to the arms of the wearer. A brightly embroidered sash, twisted several times around the waist (a little higher than is customary), with one end pendent in front, and a closely fitting linen cap, designated Masnaemphthes, completed the costume of the ordinary priest.

The vestments of the High Priest were the same as those of the lesser degrees, except that certain garments and adornments were added. Over the specially woven white linen robe the High Priest wore a seamless and sleeveless habit, sky-blue in color and reaching nearly to his feet. This was called the Meeir and was ornamented with a fringe of alternated golden bells and pomegranates. In Ecclesiasticus (one of the books rejected from the modern Bible), these bells and their purpose are described in the following words: "And he compassed him with pomegranates, and with many golden bells round about, that as he went, there might be a sound and a noise that might be heard in the temple, for a memorial to the children of his people." The Meeir was also bound in with a variegated girdle finely embroidered and with gold wire inserted through the embroidery.

81

The Ephod, a short vestment described by Josephus as resembling a coat or jacket, was worn over the upper part of the Meeir. The threads of which the Ephod was woven were of many colors, probably red, blue, purple, and white, like the curtains and coverings of the Tabernacle. Fine gold wires were also woven into the fabric. The Ephod was fastened at each shoulder with a large onyx in the form of a button, and the names of the twelve sons of Jacob were engraved upon these two stones, six on each. These onyx buttons were supposed to have oracular powers, and when the High Priest asked certain questions, they emitted a celestial radiance. When the onyx on the right shoulder was illuminated, it signified that Jehovah answered the question of the High Priest: in the affirmative, and when the one on the left gleamed, it indicated a negative answer to the query.

In the middle of the front surface of the Ephod was a space to accommodate the Essen, or Breastplate of Righteousness and Prophecy, which, as its name signifies, was also an oracle of great power. This pectoral was roughly square in shape and consisted of a frame of embroidery into which were set twelve stones, each held in a socket of gold. Because of the great weight of its stones, each of which was of considerable size and immense value, the breastplate was held in position by special golden chains and ribbons. The twelve stones of the breastplate, like the onyx stones at the shoulders of the Ephod, had the mysterious power of lighting up with Divine glory and so serving as oracles. Concerning the strange power of these flashing symbols of Israel's twelve tribes, Josephus writes:

"Yet will I mention what is still more wonderful than this: For God declared beforehand, by those twelve stones which the High Priest bare upon his breast and which were inserted into his breastplate, when they should be victorious in battle; for so great a splendor shone forth from them before the army began to march, that all the people were sensible of God's being present for their assistance. Whence it came to pass that those Greeks, who had a veneration for our laws, because they could not possibly contradict this, called the breastplate, 'the Oracle'." The writer then adds that the stones ceased to light up and gleam some two hundred years before he wrote his history, because the Jews had broken the laws of Jehovah and the God of Israel was no longer pleased with His chosen people.

The Jews learned astronomy from the Egyptians, and it is not unlikely that the twelve jewels of the breastplate were symbolic of the twelve constellations of the zodiac. These twelve celestial hierarchies were looked upon as jewels adorning the breastplate of the Universal Man, the Macroprosophus, who is referred to in the Zohar as The Ancient of Days. The number twelve frequently occurs among ancient peoples, who in nearly every case had a pantheon consisting of twelve demigods and goddesses presided over by The Invincible One, who was Himself subject to the Incomprehensible All-Father.

This use of the number twelve is especially noted in the Jewish and Christian writings. The twelve prophets, the twelve patriarchs, the twelve tribes, and the twelve Apostles—each group has a certain occult significance, for each refers to the Divine Duodecimo, or Twelvefold Deity, whose emanations are manifested in the tangible created Universe through twelve individualized channels. The secret doctrine also caught the priests that the jewels represented centers of life within their own constitutions, which when unfolded according to the esoteric instructions of the Temple, were capable of absorbing into themselves and radiating forth again the Divine light of the Deity. (The East Indian lotus blossoms have a similar meaning.) The Rabbis have taught that each twisted linen thread used in weaving the Tabernacle curtains and ornamentations consisted of twenty-four separate strands, reminding the discerning that the experience, gained during the twenty-four hours of the day (symbolized in Masonry by the twenty-four-inch rule) becomes the threads from which are woven the Garments of Glory.

THE URIM AND THUMMIM

In the reverse side of the Essen, or breastplate, was a pocket containing mysterious objects—the Urim and Thummim. Aside from the fact that they were used in divination, little is now known about these objects. Some writers contend that they were small stones (resembling the fetishes still revered by certain aboriginal peoples) which the Israelites had brought with them out of Egypt because of their belief that they possessed divine power. Others believe that the Urim and Thummim were in the form of dice, used for deciding events by being cast upon the ground. A few have maintained that they were merely sacred names, written on plates of gold and carried as talismans. "According to some, the Urim and the Thummim signify 'lights and perfections,' or 'light and truth' which last present a striking analogy to the two figures of Re (Ra) and Themi in the breastplate worn by the Egyptians." (Gardner's The Faiths of the World.)

Not the least remarkable of the vestments of the High Priest was his bonnet, or headdress. Over the plain white cap of the ordinary priest this dignitary wore an outer cloth of blue and a crown of gold, the crown consisting of three bands, one above the other like the triple miter of the Persian Magi. This crown symbolized that the High Priest was ruler not only over the three worlds which the ancients had differentiated (heaven, earth, and hell), but also over the threefold divisions of man and the universe—the spiritual, intellectual, and material worlds. These divisions were also symbolized by the three apartments of the Tabernacle itself.

At the peak of the headdress was a tiny cup of gold, made in the form of a flower. This signified that the nature of the priest was receptive and that he had a vessel in his own soul which, cuplike, was capable of catching the eternal waters of life pouring upon him from the heavens above. This flower over the crown of his head is similar in its esoteric meaning to the rose growing out of a skull, so famous in Templar symbology. The ancients believed that the spiritual nature escaping from the body passed upward through the crown of the head; therefore, the flowerlike calyx, or cup, symbolized also the spiritual consciousness. On the front of the golden crown were inscribed in Hebrew, Holiness unto the Lord.

Though robes and ornaments augmented the respect and veneration of the Israelites for their High Priest, such trappings meant nothing to Jehovah. Therefore, before entering the Holy of Holies, the High Priest removed his earthly finery and entered into the presence of the Lord God of Israel unclothed.

There he could be robed only in his own virtues, and his spirituality must adorn him as a garment.

There is a legend to the effect that any who chanced to enter the Holy of Holies unclean were destroyed by a bolt of Divine fire from the Mercy Seat. If the High Priest had but one selfish thought, he would be struck dead. As no man knows when an unworthy thought may flash through his mind, precautions had to be taken in case the High Priest should be struck dead while in the presence of Jehovah. The other priests could not enter the sanctuary therefore, when their leader was about to go in and receive the commands of the Lord, they tied a chain around one of his feet so that if he were struck down while behind the veil they could drag the body out.

THE MAGICAL WRITINGS OF THE GREAT MAGICIAN

Having lived many years free from worry and despair, it falls upon to reveal the great secrets and hidden knowledge that have been passed down to me by my forbearers. Since this knowledge has afforded me times of absolute joy and happiness, destiny compels that this happiness be shared with those deserving to learn these arcane secrets of the ancients.

Others have taken some of these great teachings and have tried to profit with books claiming to be by their own hand. But do not be taken in by these thieves of the night, their charms and incantations are tainted with the black foulness of greed and deception. The words in this fine book are indeed ancient and true of spirit, given from father to son for untold generations since the times when the angels first brought them from God's loving hand to his chosen people.

I hereby commit to the perusal of the reader a collection of great secrets, sufficient in number as may be deemed needful for any purposes. Knowing, from experience, how many an honest citizen hath been robbed of his entire estate through the machination of bad and malicious people, how many a man hath been tortured and tantalized at night, from early childhood, by wicked people of that ilk; so much so that they could hardly bear it any longer. If you are good and true of heart, the great secrets contained within this little book will release you of all troubles, whether they be troubles of this world, or the worlds of spirits both clean and unclean.

Whenever said remedy is to be applied, in case the house of him whom it is intended to assist is called aloud three times with devotion, and by adding both his Christian and all his other names, the usefulness thereof will be readily enough perceived. Thus it happens that this collection contains a number of curious performances of magic, every one of which is worth far more than the reader pays for this entire book.

For the purpose of rendering a great service to mankind, this book was issued, in order to bridle and check the doings of the spirits of wickedness. Whatever objections may be raised against this book by disbelief and jealousy, these pages will, despite all such objections, contain naught else but truth divine, since Christ himself hath commanded that all ye may perform, ye shall do in the name of God, the Son, and the Holy Spirit, so that the Devil may not possess any power over anything whatso-ever to do his will.

I, therefore, beseech every one, into whose hands this book may come, not to treat the same lightly or to destroy the same, because, by such action, he will defy the will of God. Do not use this book to gain power or take any property that belongs to someone else. Neither will you use this book to bring harm to others in any way. To do so will surely bring about the wraith of God with quick and unmerciful judgment and eternal punishment. So to him who properly esteems and values this book, and never abuses its teachings, will not only be granted the usefulness of its contents, but he will also attain everlasting joy and blessing.

Wherever the "2 N. N." occurs, both the baptismal name and all other names of him whom you intend to help, aid or assist, will have to be added, while the † † † signify the highest name of God, which should always be added in conclusion. Every sympathetic formula should be repeated three times.

A WONDERFUL PRAYER TO INSURE A HAPPY AND PROSPEROUS LIFE

Say this prayer every morning upon rising:

This grant God the Father, God the Son, and God the Holy Spirit.

Now I will rise in the name of the Lord, and will wander in his path by his word and will beseech our Savior Christ that he may lend me, upon this very day, three of his angels, for this I pray; the first he may protect me, the other keep me without weapon or arms, the third may keep my body from all harm and keep my soul, my blood and flesh, and keep my courage ever fresh. Whoever is stronger as Jesus Christ, he may approach and assail my flesh and blood. In the name of God the Father, the Son and the Holy Ghost. I praise thee heavenly host.

This may grant God the Father, God the Son, and God the Holy Spirit. † † †

BENEDICTION TO PROTECT FROM THE DANGERS OF ANY SORT OF WEAPON

Jesus, the true God and man, protect me, N. N., from all sorts of arms and weapons, be they of iron, steel, lead, or be they nails, knives or wood, whatever was made and grew since the birth of Christ, is now forged, or may yet be forged, at any future time, of whatever material. Jesus Christ, the true God and man, protect me, N. N., from murder and from cannon balls, from bullets and swords, from thunder and lightning, fire and water, chains and prison, from poison and sorcery, from mad dogs and from shedding of blood, and from sudden death. Save me, Lord God. Jesus, the true God and man, protect me, N. N., from all sorts of arms and weapons, and all those who desire to overpower me. Cause that all their might and strength to be lost, and be vain.

The Sealed Magical Book of Moses

N. N., hold and aim your armament and sword or lancet toward the cross of Christ and his sacred five wounds, in all my troubles, and at all times; and command all shot and fire-arms that they may fail to give fire; and all swords, spears, lancets, and hellebards, and other pointed instruments, that their edges may become as soft as the blood of Christ, who suffered on the cross. Jesus, protect N. N., wherever I may be, against all enemies, be they visible or invisible, secret or open. The eternal Godhead may save and protect me through the bitter sufferings, death and resurrection of Jesus Christ, and through his holy rose-colored blood, which he shed upon the cross. Jesus begotten at Nazareth, born in Bethlehem, died in Jerusalem, crucified and tortured; these are truthful words, which are written in this letter, that I may not be captured by any murderer, or any other man, be killed, whipped, wounded, nor be laid in fetters; let move away from me, or yield my will. Fly and vanish until I shall recall them, all enemies and all arms, weapons and armament, may they be called by whatever name. None will injure me. Lead and iron projectiles, remain quiet in your armament, for the sake of the martyred Jesus Christ and his holy five wounds. In the name of the Father, the Son and the Holy Spirit. In case a person has a tumor growing, or warts of any kind upon his body, he or she shall go to church and, when he notices two persons speaking to each other, he shall touch the humor or wart, and recite three times: What I see is a great sin and shame, and what I touch may vanish soon.

TO PROTECT ALL POSSESSIONS FROM THIEVES

Speak this every morning three times over all possessions:

Our dear mother in a garden came. Three angels comforted her there. The first is named St. Michael; the other, St. Gabriel; the third, St. Peter. Then spake Peter to our beloved Mary: I saw three thieves enter there. They intend to steal thy dear child and kill it. But the beloved mother Mary said: Peter, bind; St. Peter, bind; and Peter bound them with iron bands, with God's own hands, and with his holy five wounds, for this be with Gabriel, upon this day and night, and this entire year, and forever and all times, my possessions bound. Whoever attempts to steal therefrom, must stand still, like a stick, and see like a brick, and must stand quiet. He must go upward, that he cannot depart from hence until I permit him to proceed from thence. With my own tongue I must tell him this. This is my order and Gabriel's will, which now, by day and night, and all the year, for all times to come, will utter to every thief, for them to repent. For this may God his blessing lend. God the Father, God the Son, and God the Holy Spirit. Amen.

The Sealed Magical Book of Moses

PRAYER TO BE SECURED FROM ALL ASSAILANTS

Now I will Walk over the threshold I met three men, not yet very old. The first was God the Father; the other was God the Son; the third was God the Holy Spirit. They protect my body and soul, blood and flesh, that in no well I fall, that water may not swell me at all, that a rabid dog may never bite me, that shot and stone may never smite me, that spear and knife may never cut me; that never a thief may steal the least from me. Then it shall become like our dear Savior's sweat. Whoever is stronger and mightier than these three men, he may come hither, assail me if he can, or forever keep his peace with me. † † †

TO SECURE AGAINST ATTACK WHILE TRAVELING

Speak three times: *Two wicked eyes have overshadowed me, but three other eyes are overshadowing me too, the one of God, the Father, the other of God the Son, the third of God the Holy Spirit, they watch my blood and flesh, my marrow and bone, and all other large and small limbs, they shall be protected in the name of God the Holy Spirit, God the Father, God the Son.* † † †

TO PREVENT ANYONE FROM DOING EVIL AGAINST YOU

Welcome, in the name of God, ye brethren true and God, we all have drank of the Savior's blood. God the Father be with me; God the Son be with you; God the Holy Spirit be with us all. Let us meet in union and part from each other in peace. † † † *Three times spoken.*

HOW TO PREDICT THE FUTURE STATE OF THE WEATHER DURING THE YEAR

If New-Year's Day falls upon a Sunday, a quiet and gloomy winter may be expected, followed by a stormy spring, a dry summer, and a rich vintage. When New-Year's Day comes on a Monday, a varied winter, good spring, dry summer, cloudy weather, and an inferior vintage may be expected. When New-Year's comes on a Wednesday, a hard, rough winter, a blustery, dreary spring, an agreeable summer, and a blessed vintage may be hoped for. If the first of the year happens to come on Thursday, a temperate winter, agreeable spring, a dry summer, and a very good vintage will follow. If on a Friday the year begins, a changeable, irregular winter, a fine spring, a dry and comfortable summer, and a rich harvest will be the result. If New-Year's Day comes on Saturday, a rough winter, bleak winds, a wet and dreary spring, and destruction of fruit will be the consequence.

The Sealed Magical Book of Moses

TO OBTAIN MONEY

Take the eggs of a swallow, boil them, return them to the nest, and if the old swallow brings a root to the nest, take it, put it into your purse, and carry it in your pocket, and be happy.

TO OPEN ALL LOCKS

Kill a green frog, expose it to the sun for three days, powder or pulverize it. A little of this powder put into a lock will open the same.

HOW TO DISCERN ALL SECRETS AND INVISIBLE THINGS

If you find a white adder under a hazelnut shrub, which had twelve other vipers as its twelve guardsmen with it, and the hazelnut bush, under which they lay, bears commonly medlers, you must eat the white adder with your other food, and you will be enabled to see and discern all secret and otherwise hidden things.

HOW TO STOP BLEEDING

Jesus born at Bethlehem, Jesus crucified at Jerusalem, as true as these words are, to truly understand N. N. (here call the name of him whom you desire to help) that thy blood will now be stopped, in the name of God the Father, the Son, and the Holy Spirit.

HOW TO CAUSE YOUR INTENDED WIFE TO LOVE YOU

Take feathers from a rooster's tail and press them three times into her hand.

Or: Take a turtle dove tongue into your mouth, talk to your friend agreeably, kiss her and she will love you so dearly that she will never love another.

The Sealed Magical Book of Moses

WHEN YOU WISH THAT YOUR SWEETHEART SHALL NOT DENY YOU

Take the turtle dove tongue into your mouth again and kiss her, and she will accept your suit.

Or: Take salt, cheese and flour, mix it together, put it into her room, and she will rest not until she sees you.

PRAYER TO HEAL MAN AND BEAST FROM ATTACKS BY EVIL SPIRITS

Thou unclean spirit, thou has attacked N. N.; let that witchcraft recede from him into thy marrow and into thy bone, let it be returned unto thee. I exorcise thee for the sake of the five wounds of Jesus, thou evil spirit, and conjure thee for the five wounds of Jesus of this flesh, marrow and bone; I exorcise thee for the sake of the five wounds of Jesus, at this very hour restore to health again N. N., in the name of God the Father, God the Son, and of God the Holy Spirit. Speak this three times over said victim during three sunrises.

PRAYER TO FOREVER BANISH WICKED PEOPLE

All ye evil spirits, I forbid you my bedstead, my couch; I forbid you, in the name of God, my house and home; I forbid you, in the name of the Holy Trinity, my blood and flesh, my body and soul; I forbid you all the nail holes in my house and home, till you have traveled over every hillock, waded through every water, have counted all the leaflets of the trees, and counted all the starlets in the sky, until that beloved day arrives when the mother of God will bring forth her second Son. † † †

This prayer, three times spoken in the house of the bewitched person, always adding, in the right place, both his baptismal and other names, has been found excellent in many cases.

TO HEAL INJURIES ON MAN, CATTLE OR HORSE

Cut down a burdock bush, and put it into your house, so that it may wither. Then take a thread from a reel which had never been washed, and speak:

The Sealed Magical Book of Moses

Burdock bush, I bind thee that thou shalt heal the injury of this man (or beast, as the case may be), be it boils, sores, gout, swellings, or whatever it may be. Double the thread, and move around the bush, where the thickest part is, in the name of God the Father, and make a knot, then repeat the same in the name of God the Son, and make another knot, and repeat the same motion, while saying in the name of the Holy Spirit, and again make a knot, and say then: What I and thou cannot heal, that may heal the Holy Trinity.

After this, put the bush in a place where no air moves, and the injury will be healed from the root.

TO MAKE ONE'S SELF SHOT PROOF

Dig and stick mouse-ear herb on a Friday, during the half or full of the moon, tie in a white cloth and suspend it from the body. Probatum.

Or carry these words upon your body:

> *LIGHT, BETTER, CLOTENTAL,*
> *SOBATH, ADONAY,*
> *ALBOA, FLOBAT*

TO SEE WHAT OTHERS CANNOT SEE

Take a cat's eye, lay it in salt water, let it remain there for three days, and then for six days into the rays of the sun, after this have it set in silver, and hang it around your neck.

AN AMBROSE-STONE

Steal the eggs of a raven, boil them hard, lay them again into the nest and the raven will fly across the sea and bring a stone from abroad and lay it over the eggs and they will become at once soft again. If such a stone is wrapped up into a bay leaf and is given to a prisoner, that prisoner will be liberated at once. Whoever touches a door with such a stone, to him that door will be opened, and he who puts that stone into his mouth will understand the song of every bird.

The Sealed Magical Book of Moses

WHEN A CHILD IS BEWITCHED

Stand with the child toward the morning sun, and speak:

Be welcome In God's name and sunshine, from whence didst brightly beam, aid me and my dear child and feign my songs serenely stream. To keep the Father sound my praise, help praise the Holy Ghost that he restore my child to health, I praise the heavenly host. † † †

TO ALLAY PAINS WHEREVER THEY BE

Today is a holy sacred day, that God will not cause you any pain to bear, which thou may have on any part of your body, be it man, horse, cattle, or anything living, all the same. I beseech thee. Oh, holy Trinity, help this N. N., that all his pains may cease, whatever they may be called and all that Cometh from evil things. Christ commandeth, Christ vanquisheth, Christ became a being in flesh for thy sake and to protect thee against all evil. Jesus Christ of Nazareth, the crucified Saviour, with Mary his beloved mother, help this N. N. from all evil whatever name it may bear. Amen, † † †

Jesus Nazarenus Rex Judaeorum.

TO MAKE A MIRROR IN WHICH EVERYTHING MAY BE DISCERNED

Procure a looking glass, such as are commonly sold. Inscribe the characters noted below upon it. Inter it on the crossing of two pathways, during an uneven hour. On the third day thereafter, return to the place at same hour, and take it out: but you must not be the first person to look into the glass. It is best to let a dog or a cat take the first look into the mirror:

S. Solam S. Tattler S. Echogardner Gematar.

TO ASCERTAIN WHETHER OR NOT A SICK PERSON WILL DIE

Take a piece of bread, place it before the sick one's brow, then throw it before a dog. If he eats it, the patient recovers; if he rejects it, the sick one dies.

TO DRIVE AWAY AND VANQUISH ALL FOES

Whoever carries the hemlock herb, with the heart of a mole, on his person, vanquishes all his enemies, so that they will not be able to trouble him.' Such a man will obtain much. When this herb is laid under the head of a sick person, the sick one, when he sings, will get well; if he cries, he will die.

WHILE TRAVELING

Say every morning:

Grant me, oh Lord, a good and pleasant hour, that all sick people may recover, and all distressed in body or mind, repose or grace may find, and guardian angel may over them hover; and all those captive and in bondage fettered; may have their conditions and troubles bettered; to all good travelers on horse or foot, we wish a safe journey joyful and good, and good women in labor and toil a safe delivery and joy. † † †

A WAND TO DISCOVER TREASURE

Proceed in the forenoon before twelve o'clock to a hazelnut shrub, which grew within one year and has two twigs, then place yourself toward the rising sun and take the twigs in both hands and speak:

I conjure thee, one summer long, hazel rods by the power of God, by the obedience of Jesus Christ of Nazareth, God and Mary's own son, who died on the cross, and by the power of God, by the truth of God arose from the dead; God the Father, Son and Holy Ghost, who art the very truth thyself, that thou showest me where silver and gold is hidden.

The twigs will now move whenever in the presence of treasure.

HOW TO TELL A PERSON'S FORTUNE WITH CARDS

The Romany have for centuries used this method of telling fortunes with playing cards to make money off of the outsiders. Only those within the tribes know the true secrets of how to use the cards to discern the future. As many of those events about to happen may be easily gathered from the cards, I have here affixed the definition which each card in the pack bears separately; by combining them the reader must judge for himself, observing the following directions in laying them out.

It is worked with a piquet set of ordinary playing cards, which, as most people will know, consists of the usual picture-pieces and the ace, 10, 9, 8 and 7 of each suit, excluding the lower numbers.

DIAMONDS
The Ace. -Letters, or news at hand otherwise.

King. -Friendship; if followed by the Queen, marriage; if reversed, impediments, difficulties and the vexations thereto belonging.

Queen. -A woman from the country, who is fair but evil-speaking; reversed, more directly inimical to the Querent in word and also in deed.

Knave. -A postman, valet, postillion, soldier, or messenger bearing news. The news are good if the card is right side up and bad if it appears reversed. Ten. -Great joy, change of place, a party from the country.

Nine. -Delay and postponement, but not resulting in failure.

Eight. -A man of business or young merchant, who is commercially related to the Querent.

Seven. -Good news, above all if accompanied by the Ace.

HEARTS
The Ace. -Joy, contentment, and if it is accompanied by several picture-cards, marriages, feasts, etc;, in pleasant company.

King. -A rich man, banker, or financier, well disposed, and may promote the interests of the Querent. If reversed, the person is miserly and to deal with him will prove difficult.

Queen. -An honest, frank and obliging woman; if reversed, there will be some obstacle to a projected marriage.

Knave. -A soldier or young man, who is anxious to promote the Querent's welfare, will play some part in his life and will be allied with him after one or another manner.

Ten. -A surprise, but often one of a kind which will be advantageous as well as agreeable to the consulting party.

Nine. -Concord.

Eight. -Domestic and private happiness, attended by success in undertakings; exceedingly felicitous for the destinies of the middle path, the amenities of the quiet life.

Seven. -Marriage, if the Querent is a lady and the issue will be daughters only; if a man, it is destined that he will make a rich and happy marriage.

SPADES

The Ace. -In company with the ten and nine, this card signifies death, grief, more especially from bereavement, but also sorrow from many sources; it includes further the idea of treason and possibly of loss by theft or robbery.

King. -A magistrate or lawyer, whose intervention may prove disagreeable; the card reversed signifies loss in a lawsuit or general derangement of affairs.

Queen. -A disappointed woman – possibly a widow in dejection; if reversed, one who is anxious to remarry, unknown to or in spite of her family.

Knave. -Some kind of disgrace which will be inimical to the peace of mind and perhaps even the liberty of the Querent; reversed, serious complications for the person concerned; also betrayal in love, if the Querent is a woman.

Ten. -Imprisonment for a man, if followed by the Ace and King of the same suit; for a woman, disease, illness.

Nine. -Protraction and difficulties in business; followed by the Nine of Diamonds and the Ace of Clubs, delay in the receipt of expected money.

Eight. -Arrival of a person who will carry bad news if followed by the Seven of Diamonds and near to a picture card- whether King, Queen or Knave- tears, discord, destitution or loss of employment.

Seven. -Quarrels, inquietude; if ameliorated by the vicinity of some Hearts, it promises safety, independence and moral consolation.

CLUBS

The Ace. -Advantages, commercial and industrial benefits of every kind, easy collection of dues, unmixed prosperity – but these more especially when followed by the Seven of Diamonds and the Seven of Clubs.

King. -An influential, powerful person, who is equitable and benevolent towards the Querent, to whom he will render signal services; but reversed this personage will experience some difficulty in his proceedings and may be even in danger of failure.

Queen. -A dark woman, rivalry, competitive spirit; in the neighborhood of a card which stands for a man, she will have preference for the man in question; on the contrary, in proximity to a feminine card, she will be in sympathy with the Querent; reversed, she is very covetous, jealous and disposed to infidelity.

Knave. -One who is in love, a proper young man, who pays court to a young lady; placed next to a feminine card, his chances of success are very good; side by side with a man, there is reason to hope that the latter will come actively to his assistance and will contribute to his success, unless the said man should be signified by the Knave of Hearts, which presages a dangerous rivalry; reversed, there is reason to fear opposition to marriage on the part of the person's parents.

Ten. -Prosperity and good fortune of every kind; at the same time, if followed by the Nine of Diamonds a delay is foreshadowed in the return of money; contrary to all, if this card is side by side with the Nine of Spades – which everywhere signifies disappointment complete failure is promised; so also if the question at stake is a lawsuit, loss is probable.

Nine. -Success in love; for a bachelor or spinster, approaching marriage; for a widow, her second nuptials.

Eight. -A favorable conclusion which may be anticipated by the Querent in financial and business matters.

Seven. -Anxieties occasioned by love -- intrigues; followed by the Seven of Diamonds and the Nine of Spades, abundance of good things and rich family inheritances.

-SOME EXAMPLES ON HOW THE CARDS CAN BE USED -

FOR MARRIAGE AND AFFAIRS OF THE HEART

Shuffle the cards of a piquet set and cut three times. If an actual marriage is in question, remove two cards, representing the lover and the lady whose fortunes are at issue. Place these cards, face upwards, on the table before you. As usual, fair people are represented by Hearts and Diamonds but those of dark complexion by Clubs and Spades. The attribution, between these lines, seems to be usually at predilection or discretion, but Diamonds are sometimes taken to signify very fair people and blondes, while Spades are for actual brunettes and very dusky complexions.

Lay out the rest of the cards three by three; in every triplicity which produces two of the same suit, select the higher card of that suit and place it by the side of the other card which stands for the Querent. Throw out the rest for the moment, but they will be required later. When any triplicity produces entirely different suits, put aside all three in the rejected pile. When the entire cards of the set have thus been dealt with in succession, take up the rejected lot, and after shuffling and cutting as before, proceed in the same manner until you have drawn fifteen cards and placed them by the side of the Querent.

If the Querent is a dark man, he will not have his wish regarding the marriage contemplated unless a tierce to the King in Clubs be among the fifteen cards. It may of course happen that the King has been drawn to represent him. If, however; he be a Spade, then alternatively there must be a tierce in Spades. The same rule obtains if the Querent is a dark young lady, but in addition to a tierce in the suit there must be the Ace of the suit also.

If the Querent is a fair man or woman, then a tierce in the one case and a tierce and the Ace in the other must be found in Hearts or Diamonds according to the grade of their fairness. If the question concerns a marriage to take place in the country, it has been held by the expositors of the system that a tierce to the King in Diamonds is indispensable. This seems to involve the system in respect of fair people, but it is only a confusion of expression.

If Diamonds correspond to the Querent, that tierce must obviously be present, or there will be no marriage; but if present the inference is that the Querent will get his wish in respect of locality as well as of the fact of marriage. On the other hand, if the Querent is referable to any other of the three remaining suits, then ex hypothesi to attain his presumed wish for a country wedding, he must have the tierce in Diamonds as well as in his own suit.

It is not very probable that the alternative between town and country will arise as a subsidiary question, and if it does, it might be better to determine it separately by the help of some other system. It serves no purpose to ignore the shades of complexion in fair people and represent them indifferently by Diamonds, as this would be forcing the oracles and would make the reading void.

Finally, if the marriage question concerns a widower or widow, it is equally essential that the cards drawn should furnish a tierce to the King in Spades and the Ace of Hearts- which again is very hard upon all persons who are not represented by Spades. The inference is that second marriages are rare.

FOR QUESTIONS ON INHERITANCES

Shuffle and cut as before, and place on the table a card which is held to typify the Querent. The presence of the Ace of Spades, manifesting right side up, indicates profit in consequence of a death that is to say, an inheritance or legacy. If the Ace is accompanied by the Seven, Eight, Nine and Ten of Clubs, there will be a large increment of money. The combination may be difficult to secure, but very large inheritances are rarer than second marriages.

FOR LAWSUITS AND SIMILAR MATTERS

No judgment can be given on the chances of a lawsuit, actual or pending, nor generally on things of this nature, unless the King of Spades comes out in the dealing. If that card is held usually to represent the Querent, then it only follows automatically that a judgment is possible, and it is so much the easier for him in such case. The shuffling, cutting and dealing proceed as before, and if the Ace in question serves to complete the quint major in Spades – that is, the Ace, King, Queen, Knave and Ten – it is to be feared that the suit will prove good for nothing, either by going against the Querent or bringing him no profit in the opposite case. But if the Ace is accompanied by the four Tens, the chances are excellent. They are said also to be more than good in another event of the dealing which I forbear from dwelling on, as it is practically, if not otherwise, impossible for the fifteen cards – which the dealing proposes to extract – to be all of the red suits. It is well known that compilers of works on cartomancy sometimes forget the limits prescribed by their systems and get consequently into ridiculous plights.

The Sealed Magical Book of Moses

FOR A THEFT

For the discovery of a thief, the presence of the four Knaves is indispensable to any reading, and, as it happens, it is not utterly difficult – though it is none too easy – that the chances of the cards should produce them. The procedure is throughout as before. If the King and the Eight of Spades turn up among the fifteen cards, this means that the thief is already in prison; if the Ace of Spades is among them, the prisoner will be in danger of death; the presence of the Ace of Clubs, the King of Clubs and the Queen of Hearts will afford some hope that the person who stole will himself make restitution; lastly, the predominance of Diamonds offers ground for believing that the thief has been arrested, but on another charge than that which would be preferred by the Querent on his own part.

FOR A PERSON IN PRISON

The question at issue is whether the captive has any chance of speedy liberation. The procedure is throughout as before, except that the card selected is held to represent the person in durance instead of the Querent. The fifteen cards having been produced as the result of the working, they should be examined in the usual way. The presence of the Queen of Hearts, Knave of Clubs, Nine of Clubs and the four Aces will give ground for hope that liberation will be easy and at hand.

In proportion as these cards are absent, there will be delay in the desired event, and if none are found, it is likely to be rather remote. On the other hand, the appearance of the Eight and Nine of Spades, the King of Spades, and the Knave and Nine of Diamonds, will signify that liberty shall be scarcely obtained, except after many obstacles and much consequent postponement.

FOR TRAVELERS

It is assumed that the Querent is not himself on a journey but is consulting the oracles for one in whose fortunes he is for some reason interested, by ties of friendship or otherwise. Proceed as before, selecting a card to represent the absent person. When the dealing is finished, the resulting cards should be consulted to ascertain whether they include the Ace of Hearts, the Ace of Diamonds and the Ten of Diamonds, the presence of which will foreshadow probable news. Probability will be raised into certainty by the appearance of the Seven of Diamonds. If, however, the Ten of Spades is found in proximity to the card representing the person who is away on his travels, there will be reason to fear that he is ill; so also the Ace of

The Sealed Magical Book of Moses

Spades reversed will mean that he is in other danger than sickness. If he is to succeed in the enterprise that has called him abroad, he will be escorted by the Nine of Hearts, the Ace and the King of Clubs. Finally, if the Eight of Diamonds is found in relation to his own card, this means that he is on the point of returning.

There is a variation of procedure in all the above cases, which consists in protracting the dealing till twenty-one cards have been drawn instead of fifteen. It is suggested that the predominance of red cards as the result of operation in any given instance foretells great success for the person on whose behalf the consultation is made.

The Ace, Ten, Nine, Eight and Seven of Hearts are premonitory of news on which the Querent may be congratulated. The same cards in the suit of Clubs promise success in a lawsuit, or a lucky number in a lottery. The same in the suit of Spades portend news of a relative's death, or that of a friend, but whether there will be profit to the Querent is not so certain, having regard to the generally fatal nature of this suit, the constituents of which may be said almost to constitute the greater misfortunes in cartomancy. The particular numbers in the suit of Diamonds carry with them the same kind of prevision as Hearts.

These are but a few examples of what questions can be answered using the cards. One can create a simple spread of three cards representing the past, present and future that for most, is all that is needed to gain insight on one's future.

Another way is to only reverse the aces, as these are called the points, and are of most particular consequence; then take out the eights, for they are cards of no meaning; you will then nave twenty-eight left, which you must thus manage: shuffle them well, and deal them into four equal parcels; having first decided of what suit you will be the queen, and you must make your lover, or husband, of the same suit as yourself without regard to his complexion; take up the parcel dealt exactly before you, and then proceed regularly round to the right, examining them separately as you proceed. The first tells what is to happen soon, the second at some distance, and the third respects your husband or lover, and the fourth your secret wishes.

CHARMS, SPELLS AND INCANTATIONS THAT ARE TO BE RESORTED TO AT CERTAIN SEASONS OF THE YEAR, TO PROCURE BY DREAMS AN INSIGHT INTO FUTURITY, PARTICULARLY IN REGARD TO THE ARTICLE OF MARRIAGE

ST. AGNES DAY

Falls on the 21st of January; you must prepare yourself by a twenty-four hours' fast, touching nothing but pure spring water, beginning at midnight on the 20th to the same again on the 21st; then go to bed, and mind you sleep by yourself; and do not mention what you are trying to any one, or It will break the spell; go to rest on your leftside, and repeat these lines three times:

St. Agnes be a friend to me
In the gift I ask of thee;
Let me this night my husband see -

and you will dream of your future spouse. If you see more men than one in your dream, you will wed two or three times, but, if you sleep and dream not, you will never marry.

ST. MAGDALEN

Let three young women assemble together on the eve of this saint in an upper apartment, where they are sure not to be disturbed, and let no one try whose age is more than twenty-one, or it breaks the charm; get rum, wine, gin, vinegar, and water, and let each have a hand in preparing the potion. Put it in a ground-glass vessel; no other will do. Then let each young woman dip a sprig of rosemary in, and fasten It in her bosom, and, taking three sips of the mixture, get into bed; and the three must sleep together, but not a word must be spoken after the ceremony begins, and, you will have time dreams, and of such a nature that you cannot possibly mistake your future destiny. It is not particular us to the hour in which you retire to rest.

THE CHARMS OF ST. CATHERINE

This day falls on the 25th of November, and must be thus celebrated. Let any number of young women, not exceeding seven or less than three, assemble in a room, where they are sure to be safe from interlopers; just as the clock strikes eleven at night, take from your bosom a sprig of myrtle, which you must have worn there all day, and fold it up in a bit of tissue paper, then light up a small chafing dish of charcoal, and on it let each maiden throw nine hairs from her head, and a paring of her toe and finger nails, then let each sprinkle a small quantity of myrtle and frankincense in the charcoal, and while the odoriferous vapor rises, fumigate your myrtle (this plant, or tree is consecrated to Venus) with it go to bed while the clock is striking twelve, and you will be sure to dream of your future husband, and place the myrtle exactly under your head. Observe, it is no manner of use trying this charm, if you are not a real virgin, and the myrtle hour of performance must be passed in strict silence.

HOW TO MAKE YOUR LOVER OR SWEETHEART COME TO YOU

If a maid wishes to see her lover, let her take the following method. Prick the third, or wedding finger of your left hand with a sharp needle (beware a pin), and with the blood write your own and lover's name on a piece of clean writing paper in as small a compass as you can, and encircle it with three round rings of the same crimson stream, fold it up, and at exactly the ninth hour of the evening, bury it with your hand bury it within the earth, and tell no one. Your lover will hasten to you as soon as possible, and he will not be able to rest until he sees you, and if you have quarreled, to make it up. A young man may also try this charm, only instead of the wedding finger; let him pierce his left thumb,

APPLE PARINGS

On the 28th of October, which is a double Saint's day, take an apple, pare it whole, and take the paring in your right hand, and standing in the middle of the room say the following verse:

St. Simon and Jude,
On you I intrude,
By this paring I hold to discover,
Without any delay,
To tell me this day,
The first letter of my own true lover.

Turn round three times, and cast the paring over your left shoulder, and it will form the first letter of your future husband's surname; but if the paring breaks into many pieces, so that no letter is discernible, you will never marry; take the pips of the same apple, put them in spring water, and drink them.

TO KNOW HOW SOON A PERSON WILL BE MARRIED

Get a green pea-pod, in which are exactly nine peas, hang it over the door, and then take notice of the next person who comes in, who is not of the family, and if it proves a bachelor, you will certainly be married within that year.

On any Friday throughout the year – take rosemary flowers, bay leaves, thyme, and sweet marjoram, of each a handful; dry these and make them into a fine powder; then take a tea-spoon-fill of each sort, mix the powders together; then take twice the quantity of barley flour and make the whole into cake with the milk of a red cow. This cake is not to be baked, but wrapped in clean writing paper, and laid under your head any Friday night. If the person dreams of music, she will wed those she desires, and that shortly; if of fire, she will be crossed in love; if of a church, she will die single. If any thing is written or the least spot of ink is on the paper, it will not do.

TO KNOW WHAT FORTUNE YOUR FUTURE HUSBAND WILL BE

Take a walnut, a hazel-nut, and nutmeg; grate them together, and mix them with butter and sugar, and make them up into small pills, of which exactly nine must be taken on going to bed; and according to her dreams, so will be the state of the person she will marry. If a gentleman, of riches; if a clergyman, of white linen; if a lawyer, of darkness; if a tradesman, of odd noises and tumults; if a soldier or sailor, of thunder and lightning; if a servant, of rain.

A CHARM FOR DREAMING

When you go to bed, place under your pillow a Common Prayer Book, open at the part of the Matrimonial service, in which is printed, "With this ring I thee wed," etc., place on a key, a ring, a flower and a sprig of willow, a small heart cake, a crust of bread, and the following cards, the ten of clubs, nine of hearts, ace of spades, and the ace of diamonds; wrap all these round in a handkerchief of thin gauze or muslin, on getting into bed cram your hoods and say:

Luna ever woman's friend,

The Sealed Magical Book of Moses

To me thy goodness condescend;
Let me this night in visions see,
Emblems of my destiny.

If you dream of storms, trouble will betide you; if the atom ends in a fine calm, so will your fate; if of a ring, or of the act of diamonds, marriage; bread, an industrious life; cake, a pros perous life; flowers, joy; willow, treachery in love; spades, death; diamonds, money; clubs, a foreign land; hearts, illegitimate children; keys, that you will rise to great trust and power, and never know want; birds, that you will have many children, geese, that you will marry more than once.

THE FLOWER AUGURY

If a young man or woman receives a present of flowers, or a nosegay from, their sweetheart, unsolicited, for if asked for, it destroys the influence of the spell; let them keep them in the usual manner in cold water four-and-twenty hours, then shift the water, and let them stand another twenty-four hours, then take them, and immerse the stalks in water nearly boiling, leave them to perish for three hours, then look at them; if they are perished, or drooping, your lover is false; if revived and blooming, you will be happy in your choice.

HOW TO TELL BY A SCREW, WHETHER YOUR SWEETHEART LOVES YOU OR NOT

Get a small screw, such as the carpenters use for hanging closet-doors, and after making a hole in a plank with a gimlet of a proper size, put the screw in, being careful to oil the end with a little sweet oil. After having done this, take a screw-driver and drive the screw home, but you must be sure and observe how many turns it takes to get the screw in so far that it will go no farther. If it requires an odd number of turns you can rest assured that your sweetheart does not love you yet, and perhaps is enamored of some other person; but if the number of turns is an even number, be happy, for your sweetheart adores you, and lives only in the sunshine of your presence.

STRANGE BED

Lay under your pillow a prayer-book, opened at the Matrimonial Service, bound round with the garters you wore that day and a sprig of myrtle, on the page that says, "with this ring I thee wed," and your dream will be ominous, and you will have your fortune as well told as if you had paid a crown to an astrologer.

A SPELL
(To be used at any convenient time)

Make a nosegay of various colored flowers, one of a sort, a sprig of rue. and some yarrow off a grave, and bind all together with the hair from your head; sprinkle them with a few drops of the oil of amber, using your left hand, and bind the flowers round your head under your night-cap when you retire to rest; put on clean sheets and linen, and your future mate will appear in your dream.

PROMISE OF MARRIAGE

If you receive a written one, or any declaration to that effect in a letter, prick the words with a sharp-pointed needle on a sheet of paper quite clear from any writing; fold in nine folds, and place it under your head when you retire to rest. If you dream of diamonds, castles, or even a clear sky, there is no deceit and you will prosper. Trees in blossom, or flowers, show children; washing, or graves, show you will lose them by death; and water shows they are faithful, but that you will go through severe poverty with the party for some time, though all may end well.

TO KNOW YOUR HUSBAND'S TRADE

Exactly at twelve, on Midsummer-day, place a bowl of water in the sun, pour in some boiling pewter as the clock is striking, saying:

Here I try a potent spell, Queen of love and Juno tell, In kind love to me, What my husband Is to be; This the day, and this the hour. When it seems you have the power or to be a maiden's friend. So, good ladies, condescend.

A tobacco-pipe full is enough. When the pewter is cold, take it out of the water, and drain it dry in a cloth, and you will find the emblems of your future husband's trade quite plain. If more than one, you will marry-twice; if confused and no emblems, you will never marry; a coach shows a gentleman for you.

The Sealed Magical Book of Moses

A CHRISTMAS SPELL

Steep mistletoe berries, to the number of nine, in a mixture of ale, wine, vinegar, and honey; take them on going to bed, and you will dream of your future lot; a storm in this dream is very bad; it is most likely that you will marry a sailor, who will suffer shipwreck at sea; but to see either sun, moon, or stars is an excellent presage; so are flowers; but a coffin is an unfortunate index of a disappointment in love.

THE NINE KEYS

Get nine small keys; they must all be your own by begging or purchase (borrowing will not do, nor must you tell what you want them for); plait a three-plaited braid of your own hair, and tie them together, fastening the ends with nine knots; fasten them with one of your garters to your left wrist on going to bed, and bind the other garter round your head; then say:

St. Peter take it not amiss, To try your favor I've done this; You are the ruler of the keys, Favor me, then, if you please; Let me then your influence prove, And see my dear and wedded love.

This must be done on the eve of St. Peter's. It is an old charm used by the maidens of Rome In ancient times, who put great faith in it.

THE THREE KEYS

Purchase three small keys, each at a different place, and, on going to bed, tie them together with your garter, and place them in your left hand glove, along with a small flat dough cake, on which you have pricked the first letters of your sweetheart's name; put them on your bosom when you retire to rest; if you are to have that young man, you will dream of him, but not else.

TO KNOW IF A WOMAN WITH CHILD WILL HAVE A GIRL OR A BOY

Write the proper names of the father and the mother, and the mouth she conceived with child; count the letters in these words, and divide the amount by seven; and then, if the remainder be even, it will be a girl; if uneven, it will be a boy.

The Sealed Magical Book of Moses

TO KNOW IF A CHILD NEW-BORN SHALL LIVE OR NOT

Write the proper names of the father and mother, and of the day the child was born; count the letters in these words, and to the amount add twenty-five, and then divide the whole by seven; if the remainder be even, the child shall die, but if it be uneven, the child shall live.

A CHARM
(To be used on the eve of any fast directed in the calendar)

This takes a week's preparation, for you must abstain from meat or strong drink. Go not to bed till the clock has struck the midnight hour, and rise before seven the next morning, the whole seven days. You must neither play at cards, or any game of chance, nor enter a place of public diversion. When you go to bed on the night of trial, eat something very salty, and do not drink after it, and you may depend on having very singular dreams; and, being very thirsty, you will probably dream of liquids. Wine is excellent, and shows wealth or promotion; brandy, foreign lands; rum, that you will wed a sailor, or one that gets his living at sea; gin, but a middling life; cordials, variety of fortune; and water, if you drink it, poverty; but to see a clear stream is good. Children are not good to behold in this dream, nor cards, nor dice; they forebode the loss of reputation, or that you will never marry.

VALENTINE

If you receive one of those love tokens, and cannot guess at the party who sent it, the following method will explain it to a certainty. Prick the fourth finger on your left hand, and, with a crow quill, write on the back of the valentine the year, day and hour on which you were born, also the present year. Try this on the first Friday after you receive the valentine, but do not go to bed till midnight; place the paper in your left shoe, and put it under your pillow; lay on your left side, and repeat three times:

St. Valentine, pray condescend To be this night a maiden's friend; Let me now my lover see. Be he of high or low degree; By a sign his station show, Be it weal or be it woe; Let him come to my bedside, And my fortune thus decide.

The young woman will be sure to dream of the identical person who sent the valentine, and may guess, by the other particulars of the dream, if or not he is to be her spouse.

The Sealed Magical Book of Moses

YARROW

This is a weed commonly found in abundance on graves towards the close of the spring and beginning of the summer. It must be plucked exactly on the first hour of morn; place three sprigs either in your shoe or glove, saying:

Good morning, good morning, good yarrow, And thrice a good morning to thee; Tell me before this time tomorrow Who my true love is to be.

Observe, a young man must pluck the weed off a young maiden's grave, and a female must select that of a bachelor's; retire home to bed without speaking a word, or it dissolves the spell; put the yarrow under your pillow, and it will procure a sure dream, on which you may depend.

TO KNOW WHETHER A WOMAN SHALL HAVE THE MAN SHE WISHES

Get two lemon peels and wear them all day, one in each pocket, and at night rub the four posts of the bedstead with them; if she Is to succeed, the person will appear in her sleep, and present her with a couple of lemons; if not, there Is no hope.

TO KNOW IF ANYONE SHALL ENJOY THEIR LOVE OR NOT

Take the number of the first letter of your name, the number of the planet, and the day of the week; put all these together, and divide them by thirty; if it be above, it will come to your mind, and if below, to the contrary; and mind that number which exceeds not thirty.

SIGNS TO CHOOSE GOOD HUSBANDS AND WIVES

1. If the party be of a ruddy complexion, high and full-nosed, his eyebrows bending arch-wise, his eyes standing full, of a black and lively color, it denotes him good-natured, ingenious, and born to good fortune, and the like in a woman, if born under the planet Jupiter.

2. If the party be phlegmatic, lean, and of a dusky complexion, given much to musing and melancholy, beware of such a one, of what sex soever.

3. An indifferent wide mouth, and full cheeks, smooth forehead, little ears, dark-brown hair, and a chin proportionate to the face, is very promising.

4. An extraordinarily long chin, with the underlip larger than the upper, signifies a cross-grained person, fit for little business, yet given to folly.

5. A well-set, broad chin in a man, his face being round, and not too great, and a dimple or dent in a woman's cheek or chin denotes they will come together and live happily.

PREDICTIONS CONCERNING CHILDREN BORN ON ANY DAY OF THE YEAR

SUNDAY-The child born on Sunday will obtain great riches, be long-lived, and enjoy much happiness.

MONDAY-Children born on this day will not be very successful in most enterprises they may engage in, being irresolute, subject to be imposed upon through their good-natured disposition; they are generally willing and ready to oblige every one who asks a favor from them.

TUESDAY-The person born on this day will be subject to violent starts of passion, and not easily reconciled; if a man, given to illicit connections, from which conduct many serious consequences and misfortunes will arise, and lie will never be safe, being in danger of suffering death by violence, if lie does not put a restraint upon his vicious inclinations.

WEDNESDAY-The child ushered into the world on this day will be of a studious and sedate turn of mind; and if circumstances will allow, fond of perusing the literary works of the most talented ancient and modern authors. Should facilities be afforded to such a one, there is every probability of his being a highly-gifted author.

THURSDAY-Those who first see the light on this day may in general have applied to them the appellation of being "born with a silver spoon in their mouths"; for unless they resolutely spurn from them the Plutonic deity, riches will be poured into their lap with no discerning hand.

FRIDAY-The little stranger who first inhales the vital air on this day will be blessed with a strong constitution, and will be lucky in every enterprise through life, happy in his or her domestic relations, and finally die rich and lamented.

SATURDAY-This is an unlucky day for being ushered into this world of sin and sorrow; but those born on this last day of the week may become good members of society, honored and respected by their fellow-creatures, and blessed by the Almighty.

TO DISCOVER A THIEF BY THE SIEVE AND SHEAR

Stick the points of the shears In the wood of the sieve, and let two persons support it, balanced upright, with their two fingers; then read a certain chapter in the Bible, and afterwards ask St. Peter and St. Paul if A or B is the thief, naming all the persons you suspect. On naming the real thief, the sieve will suddenly turn round about.

SIGN OF A SPEEDY MARRIAGE AND SUCCESS ATTENDING IT BY SUNDAY SIGNS

1. For a woman to have the first and last letters of her Christian name the same with the man's surname that makes love to her denotes a great union and a generous love.

2. For a man to have the first and last letters of his Christian name the same with the woman's surname denotes the some.

3. To think on a party on a sudden awaking, without any meditation, on a Friday morning that before had a place in the affection of man or woman is a demonstration of love or extraordinary friendship.

4. If a ring falls accidentally off a man's finger that is under no obligation of marriage and runs directly to the feet of a maid or widow, it denotes that he is not only in love with the widow, but that a sudden marriage will ensue.

5. The singing of a robin red-breast at your window, in the time of courtship, on a Wednesday, is a sign that you shall have the party desired.

6. If when walking abroad with your sweetheart, you perceive a pair of pigeons circle you round, it is a sign of marriage and happiness to ensue, with much content.
7. If a hare cross you on a Saturday morning, it promises happy days, riches, and pleasure.

ANCIENT METHODS TO KNOW THE WEATHER

In the evening when the horizon in the West is tinged with a ruddy glow, it is a sign that bright and dry weather will speedily follow.

When the sky appears ruddy in the East in the evening, changeable weather may be confidently anticipated.

Should the horizon in the North wear a ruddy appearance in the evening, stormy and boisterous weather may be expected.

When the rays from the sun at mid-day are more than ordinarily dazzling, rainy weather will shortly succeed.

In summer time, when the swallows fly near to the ground, rainy weather will assuredly soon follow.

The shrill crowing of the cock during rainy weather is a sign that drought will speedily prevail.

When the smoke from the chimney falls down towards the ground, instead of rising upwards, it is a sign that rainy weather will soon follow.

When the face of the moon is partially obscured by a light thin vapor, rain will shortly follow.

If on a foggy morning in. summer the fog rises upwards, it will be a fine day; if the fog falls to the ground, it will be wet.

When you see the fowls in a farm-yard flocking together under some covert, be assured that ungenial weather is about to succeed.

When the rooks, on flying over your head, make an extraordinary and discordant cawing, rain will come on shortly.

When you see your dog or cat more than ordinarily restless, frisking about the house in all directions, be assured that some boisterous weather will shortly succeed.

In rainy weather, when you hear the chirping of the sparrows on the house-top more shrill than usual, it is a sign that clear and dry weather will quickly succeed.

The Sealed Magical Book of Moses

When you see a vapory fluid resting upon a stagnant pond on the forepart of the day, you may conclude that rainy weather will shortly come on. Should the vapor ascend and clear away, a continued drought may be anticipated.

In summer, when the atmosphere is dense and heavy, and there is scarcely a breath of air, be assured that a thunderstorm is coming on.

When the firmament is lighted up with meteoric phenomena, such as failing stars, globes of fire, etc., changeable and boisterous weather may be expected to prevail.

When the rising sun appears like a solid mass of fervent-heated metal, and no rays appear to emanate there from, fine and dry weather may be confidently anticipated.

When the sun sets in a halo of ruddy brightness, genial and bright weather may be fully relied on for the coming day.

When the moon appears of a ruddy hue, stormy and boisterous weather may be expected to follow.

When the stars appear of a sparkling brightness, fine and genial weather may be expected to prevail for some time. Should the stars appear obscure and dim, changeable and rainy weather may be anticipated.

When, in summer time, yon see the cattle grazing in a field gathering together in groups, be assured that a thunder-storm is approaching.

The luminous appearance of the Aurora Borealis, or Northern Lights, foretells the approach of stormy and boisterous weather.

When the Betting sun in the autumn or winter seasons appears ruddy, it is a sign that high and boisterous winds may be expected to blow from, the North and Northwest. When the sun at its rising in the autumn or winter seasons appears ruddy, it foretells that high and boisterous winds may be anticipated to blow from the South and Southeast

When the sea-birds are observed flocking towards the shore, storms and tempests may be confidently expected.

When, in the early autumn season, the migratory birds are seen flocking together, and raking their departure, it is a certain sign that rough and boisterous weather is approaching, and that a severe winter may be anticipated.

When the doves around a dove-cote make a more than ordinary cooing, and frequently pass in and out of their cote, it is a sign that a change of weather is near. When the robin approaches your habitation, it is a sign that wintry weather will shortly prevail.

When there is a thick vapory mist resting on the tops of high hills in the morning, and remains there during the day, it is a sign that wet and ungenial weather may be anticipated, should the mist eventually rise upward, and be evaporated by the sun's rays, a return to fine, dry weather may be looked for; if, how-aver, the mist falls down into the valley, a continuation of wet weather will prevail.

SIGNS AND OMENS: AUGURIES AND FOREWARNINGS

However skeptical some persons may pro fess to be on the subject of signs, auguries, and forewarnings, still few will venture to deny that in innumerable instances those mysterious admonitions and forewarnings have been speedily followed by events of a pleasant or a painful nature to those who have received them. The belief in signs and auguries has been cherished by mankind ever since the creation; and this faculty is not confined to the human family alone, but the lower animals possess some of them in an extraordinary degree. The following are a few of the multifarious signs and auguries which admonish and forewarn mankind, at one time or another:

Should you be the subject of a deep depression of spirits, contrary to your usual constitutional buoyancy and liveliness, it is a sign that you are about to receive some agreeable intelligence.

If the crown of your head itches more than ordinary, you may expect to be advanced to a more honorable position in life. Should the hair on your head come off, when combing, in greater quantities than usual, it is a sign that you will soon be the subject of a severe attack of affliction.

If your right eyebrow should immoderately itch, be assured that you are going to look upon a pleasant sight - a long-absent friend, or a long-estranged, but now reconciled, lover.

Should your left eyebrow be visited with a tantalizing itching, it is a sign that you will soon look upon a painful sight – the corpse of a valued friend, or your lover walking with a favored rival.

The Sealed Magical Book of Moses

A ringing in your right ear is an augury that you will shortly hear some pleasant news.

A ringing in your left ear is a sign that you will in a short time receive intelligence of a very unpleasant nature. When your left ear tingles some one is back-biting you.
A violent itching of the nose foretells trouble and sorrow to those who experience it.

An itching of the lips in a sign that some one is speaking disrespectfully of you.

When you are affected by an itching on the back of your neck, be assured that either yourself or some one nearly related to you is about to suffer a violent death.

An itching on the right shoulder signifies that you will shortly have a large legacy bequeathed to you.

When you feel an itching sensation on your left shoulder, be sure that you are about to bear a heavy burden of sorrow and trouble.

If your right elbow joint itches, you may expect shortly to hear some intelligence that will give you extreme pleasure.

Should you be annoyed with a violent itching on your left elbow joint, you may be sure that some vexatious disappointment will be experienced by you,

If you feel an itching on the palm of your right hand, you may expect soon to receive some money which you have been long expecting.

When the palm of your left hand itches, you may expect to be called upon to pay some money for a debt which you have not personally incurred.

An itching on the spine of your back is a sign that you will shortly be called upon to bear a heavy burden of sorrow and trouble.
An itching on your loins is an indication that you will soon receive an addition to your family, if married; if single, that you are on the eve of marriage.

When you are affected with an itching on the belly; expect to be invited to feast upon a choice collection of savory meats.

When either or both of your thighs itch, be assured that you are about to change your sleeping apartment.

The Sealed Magical Book of Moses

If you have an itching sensation in your right knee, depend upon it that you will shortly undergo a remarkable and beneficial change in your previous course of life, and become religiously inclined.

If a similar sensation prevails in your right knee, you may expect to undergo a change in your deportment of an unfavorable nature.

An itching sensation on the shins foretells that you will be visited with a painful and long-continued affliction.

When your ankle-joints itch, be sure that you are about to be united to one whom you love, if single; if married, that your domestic comforts will be largely increased.

When the sole of your right foot itches, you may feel assured that you are about to undertake a journey from which you will derive much pleasure and enjoyment.

Should you experience a similar sensation on the sole of your left foot, you may expect to be called upon to take a journey of an unpleasant and melancholy nature.

If, in taking a walk, you should see a single magpie, it is a bad omen, especially if it should fly past you to the left hand; but if it should pass you to the right hand, the good will counterbalance the bad. Should you see two magpies together, expect to hear of something to your advantage – a proposal of marriage, if single; or a legacy of money bequeathed to you. Should the magpies fly past you together to your right hand, your own marriage, or the marriage of some one nearly related to you, will occur in a short time. The seeing of several magpies together is considered a very fortunate omen.

May is considered an unlucky month to marry in; therefore avoid doing so if possible. If you can catch a snail by the horns on the first of May, and throw it over your shoulders, you will be lucky throughout the year. If you place one on a slate on that day, it will describe by its turnings the initials of your future partner's name.

If a young man or young woman, on going up a flight of stairs, should stumble in the middle of the flight, it is a sign that his or her marriage will take place in a short time. If the stumbling should be near the top of the stairs, then his or her marriage will be immediately consummated.

If a young person, when seated at the tea-table, should observe one or more stalks of the tea-plant in the newly-poured-out cup, and if, on stirring the tea and holding the spoon in the middle of the liquid, the stalk or stalks should come close to the spoon handle, it is a token that he or she will be soon married.

When the house-dog is unusually restless, and howls dismally in the night-time, it is a sign that sickness and death are about to visit the family to whom the dog belongs.

When the wick of your candle shows a bright spark in the midst of the flame, it is a sign that a long-absent friend is about to visit you.

When the ribs of your fire-grate are more than usually covered with flukes of soot, it is a sign that a stranger is about to visit your habitation.

If a person stumbles when leaving his house at the beginning of a journey, or trips or stumbles more than once during the course of the journey, it is advisable to postpone it.

It is bad luck to sweep the kitchen floor after dark, and you are sweeping out good luck if you sweep dirt out the door.

If you burn beef bones by mistake it is a sign of much sorrow to come on account of poverty. To burn fish or poultry bones indicates that scandal will be spread about you.

To cross two forks accidentally is a sign that slander will be spread about you. To stir anything with a fork is to stir up misfortune. As well, crossing two table-knives by accident portends bad luck.

To be completely naked in your dream is a very lucky omen. If only your feet are bare, you will have many difficulties to overcome before you can reach your goal. Also, to dream of someone smoking a cigar indicates that money is on its way.

If you involuntarily make a rhyme, that is a lucky omen. Before speaking again, make a wish, and the chances are that it will come true.

It is a sign of good luck if you first see the new moon over your left shoulder, but of bad luck if you see it over your right. Should you have money in your pocket at the time of the new moon, you will be penniless before the moon is in the full.

To sneeze three times in rapid succession is considered by some to be a good omen.

It is a sure sign that your plans will meet with success if three bees alight on you at the same time.

If you find a coin, you should spit on it to bring good luck.

If the palm of the left hand itches you will be getting money; if the right palm itches, you will be losing/spending money.

A dog passing between a couple about to be married means ill fortune will befall the couple. However, being followed by a strange dog indicates good luck.

FORTUNE TELLING BY THE GROUNDS IN A TEA OR COFFEE CUP

Pour the grounds of tea or coffee into a white cup; shake them well about, so as to spread them over the surface; reverse the cop to drain away the superfluous contents, and then exercise jour fertile fancy in discovering what the figures thus formed represent Long, wavy lines denote vexatious and losses-their importance depending on the number of lines. Straight ones, on the contrary, foretell peace, tranquility, and long life.

Human figures are usually good omens, announcing love affairs, and marriage.

If circular figures predominate, the person for whom the experiment is made may expect to receive money. If these circles are connected by straight, unbroken lines, there will be delay, but ultimately all will be satisfactory, Squares, foretell peace and happiness; oblong figures, family discord; whilst curved, twisted, or angular ones, are certain signs of vexations and annoyances, their probable duration being determined by the number of figures.

A crown signifies honor; a cross, news of death; a ring, marriage-if a letter can be discovered near it that will be the initial of the name of the future spouse. If the ring is in the clear part of the cup, it foretells happy union; if clouds are about it, the contrary; but if it should chance to be quite at the bottom, then the marriage will never take place.

A leaf of clover, or trefoil, is a good sign, denoting, if at the top of the cup, speedy good fortune, which will be more or less distant in case it appears at, or Dear the bottom.

The Sealed Magical Book of Moses

The anchor, if at the bottom of the cup, denotes success in business; at the top, and in the clear part, love and fidelity; but in thick, or cloudy parts, inconstancy.

The serpent is always the sign of an enemy, and if in the cloudy part, gives warning that great prudence will be necessary to ward off misfortune.

The coffin portends news of a death, or long illness.

The dog, at the top of the cup, denotes true and faithful friends; in the middle, that they are not to be trusted; but at the bottom, that they are secret enemies.

The lily, at the top of the cup, foretells a happy marriage; at the bottom, anger.

A letter signifies news; if in the dear, very welcome ones; surrounded by dots, a remittance of money; but if hemmed in by clouds, bad tidings, and losses. A heart near it denotes a love letter. A single portends restoration to health; a group of trees in the dear; misfortunes, which may be avoided; several trees, wide apart, promise that your wishes 'will be accomplished; if encompassed by dashes, it is a token that your fortune is in its blossom, and only requires care to bring to maturity; if surrounded by dots, riches.

Mountains signify either friends or enemies, according to their situation.

The sun, moon, and stars, denote happiness, success. The clouds, happiness or misfortune, according as they are bright or dark.

Birds are good omens, but quadrupeds-with the exception of the dog-foretell trouble and difficulties.

Fish; imply good news from across the water.

A triangle portends an unexpected legacy; a single straight line, a journey.

The figure of a man, indicates a speedy visitor; if the arm is outstretched, a present; when the figure is very distinct, it shows that the person expected will be of dark complexion, and vice versa.

A crown, near a cross, indicates a large fortune, resulting from a death.

Flowers are signs of joy, happiness, and peaceful life.

A heart, surrounded by dots, signifies joy, occasioned by the receipt of money; with a ring near it, approaching marriage.

HOW TO READ YOUR FORTUNE BY THE WHITE OF AN EGG

Break a new-laid egg, and, carefully separating the yolk from the white, drop the latter into a large tumbler half full of water; place this, uncovered, in some dry place, and let it remain untouched for four-and-twenty hours, by which time the white of the egg will have formed itself into various figures-rounds, squares, ovals, animals, trees, crosses, which are to be interpreted in the same manner as those formed by the coffee grounds. Of course, the more whites there are in the glass, the more figures there will be.

This is a very interesting experiment, and much practiced by the young Scotch maidens, who, however, believe it to have more efficacies when tried on either Midsummer Eve or Halloween.

USING AN EGG TO REMOVE BAD LUCK

If you are plagued by evil spells and bad luck, try this powerful, ancient spell to help you remove any bewitchment from your life.

You must purchase a brown fresh egg before noon of that day. Make sure that you start this when the moon is waning. It is very important that this egg be fresh. Place this egg in a brown bag and tie the neck of the bag with a black cloth string. Place this bag under your bed.

Each night before retiring to bed, you must open this bag and take the egg out and rub it all over your body. When done, put the egg back into the bag, take a deep breath and blow three times into the bag. When you are blowing into the bag, you must imagine that all the bad luck is leaving your body through your breath.

When done, place the bag back under your bed. Do this for nine days. At the end of nine days, take the bag with the egg and dispose of it outside your home.

Each time that you blow into the bag, you must immediately tie it back up. If by the end of seven days you notice that your bag is moving on its own. Stop, and dispose of the bag immediately. Do not look into the bag and make sure that the bag is secure.   Only do this if you are serious about removing bad luck and evil bewitchments in your life.

HOW TO TELL FORTUNES BY THE MOLES ON A PERSON'S BODY

1. A mole that stands on the right side of the forehead, or tight temple, signifies that the person will arrive to sudden wealth and honor.

2. A mole on the right eyebrow, announces speedy marriage, the husband to possess many good qualities and a large fortune.

3. A mole on the left of either of those three places, portends unexpected disappointment in your most sanguine wishes.

4. A mole on the outside of either eye, denotes the person to be of a steady, sober, and sedate disposition.

5. A mole on either cheek, signifies that the person never shall rise above mediocrity in point of fortune.

6. A mole on the nose, shows that the person will have good success in his or her undertakings.

7. A mole on the lip, either upper or lower, proves the person to be fond of delicate things, and much given to the pleasures of love, in which he or she will most commonly be successful.

8. A mole on the chin, indicates that the person will be attended with great prosperity, and be highly esteemed.

9. A mole on the side of the neck, shows that the person will narrowly escape suffocation; but will afterward rise to great consideration by an unexpected legacy or inheritance.

10. A mole on the throat, denotes that the person shall become rich, by marriage.

11. A mole on the right breast, declares the person to be exposed to a sudden reverse from comfort to distress, by unavoidable accidents. Most of his children will be girls.

12. A mole on the left breast, signifies success in undertakings and an amorous disposition. Most of his children will be boys.

13. A mole on the bosom, portends mediocrity of health and fortune.

14. A mole under the left breast, over the heart, foreshows that a man will be of a warm disposition, unsettled in mind, fond of rambling, and light in his conduct. In a lady it shows sincerity in love, and easy travail in child-birth.

15. A mole on the right side over any part of the ribs, denotes the person to be pusillanimous, and slow in understanding any thing that may be attended with difficulties.

16. A mole on the belly, shows the person to be addicted to sloth and gluttony, and not very choice in point of dress.

17. A mole on either hip, shows that the person will have many children, and that they will be healthy and possess much patience.

18. A mole on the right thigh, is an indication of riches, and much happiness in the married state.

19. A mole on the left thigh, denotes poverty and want of friends through the enmity and injustice of others.

20. A mole on the right knee, shows the person will be fortunate In the choice of a partner for life, and meet with few disappointments in the world.

21. A mole on the left knee, portends that the person will be rash, inconsiderate, and hasty, but modest when in cool blood.

22. A mole on either leg, shows that the person is indolent, thoughtless, and indifferent as to whatever may happen.

23. A mole on either ankle, denotes a man to be inclined to effeminacy and elegance of dress; a lady to be courageous, active and industrious, with a trifle of the termagant.

24. A mole on either foot, forebodes sudden illness or unexpected misfortune.

25. A mole on the right shoulder, indicates prudence, discretion, secrecy, and wisdom.

26. A mole on the left shoulder, declares a testy, contentious, and ungovernable spirit.

27. A mole on the right arm, denotes vigor and courage.

28. A mole on the left arm, declares resolution and victory in battle.

29. A mole near either elbow, denotes restlessness, a roving and unsteady temper, also a discontentedness with those which they are obliged to live constantly with.

30. A mole between the elbow and the wrist, promises the person prosperity, but not until he has undergone many hardships.

31. A mole on the wrist, or between it, and the ends of the fingers, shows industry, parsimony, and conjugal affection.

32. A mole on any part, from the shoulders to the loins, is indicative of imperceptible decline and gradual decay, whether of health or wealth.

LIST OF UNLUCKY DAYS, WHICH, TO FEMALES BORN ON THEM, WILL GENERALLY PROVE UNFORTUNATE

January 6, 6, 13, 14, 20, and 21.
February 2, 3, 9, 10, 16, 17, 22, and 23.
March I, 2, 8, 9, 16, 17, 28, and 29.
April 24 and 25,
May 1, 2, 9, 17, 22, 29, and 30.
June 5, 6, 12, 13, 18, and 19
July 3 and 4.
September 9 and 16.
October 20 and 27.
November 9, 10, 21, 29, and 30
December 6, 14, and 21.

I particularly advise all females born on these days to be extremely cautious of placing their affections too hastily, as they will be subject to disappointments and vexations in that respect; it will be better for them (in those matters) to be guided by the advice of their friends, rather than by their own feelings, they will be less fortunate in placing their affections, than in any other action of their lives, as many of these marriages will terminate in separations, divorces, etc. Their courtships will end in elopements, seductions, and other ways not necessary of explanation.

My readers must be well aware that affairs of importance begun at inauspicious times, by those who have been born at those periods when the stars shed their malign influence, can seldom, if ever, lead to much good: it is, therefore, that I endeavor to lay before them a correct statement drawn from accurate astrological information, in order that by strict attention and care, they may avoid falling into those perplexing labyrinths from which nothing but that care and attention can save them.

The list of days I have above given will be productive of hasty and clandestine marriages – marriages under untoward circumstances, perplexing attachments, and, as a natural consequence, the displeasure of friends, together with family dissensions, and division.

LIST OF DAYS USUALLY CONSIDERED FORTUNATE

With respect to Courtship, Marriage and Love affairs in general - females that were born on the following days may expect Court ships and prospects of Marriage which will have a happy termination.

January 1, 2, 15, 26, 27, 28.
February 11, 21, 26, 26.
March 10, 24.
April 6, 15, 16, 20, 28.
May 3, 13, 18, 31.
June 10, 11, 15, 22, 25.
July 9, 14, 15, 28.
August 6, 7, 10, 11, 16, 20, 25.
September 4, 8, 9, 17, 18, 23.
October 3, 7, 16, 21, 22.
November 5, 14, 20.
December 14, 15, 19, 20, 22, 23, 25.

Although the greater number, or indeed nearly all the ladies that are born on the days stated in the preceding list, will be likely to meet with a prospect of marriage, or become engaged in some love affair of more than ordinary importance, yet it must not be expected that the result will be the same with all of them; with some they will terminate in marriage with others in disappointment and some of them will be in danger of forming attachments that may prove of a somewhat troublesome description.

I shall, therefore, in order to enable my readers to distinguish them, give a comprehensive and useful list, showing which of them will be most likely to marry. Those born within the limits of the succeeding List of Hours, on any of the preceding days, will be the most likely to marry or win, at least, have Courtships that will be likely to have a happy termination.

THE MOON
JUDGMENTS DRAWN FROM THE MOON'S AGE

1. A child born within twenty-four hours after the new moon will be fortunate and live to a good old ace. Whatever is dreamt on that day will be fortunate and pleasing to the dreamer.

2. The second day is very lucky for discovering things lost, or hidden treasure; the child born on this day shall thrive.

3. The child born on the third day will be fortunate through persons in power, and whatever is dreamed will prove true.

4. The fourth day is bad; persons falling sick on this day rarely recover.

5. The fifth day is favorable to begin a good work, and the dreams will be tolerably successful; the child born on this day will be vain and deceitful.

6. The sixth day the dreams will not immediately come to pass and the child born will not live long.

7. On the seventh day do not tell your dreams, for much depends on concealing them; if sickness befalls you on this day, you will soon recover; the child born will livelong, but have many troubles.

8. On the eighth day the dreams will come to pass; whatever business a person undertakes on this day will prosper.

9. The ninth day differs very little from the former; the child born on this day will arrive at great riches and honor.

10. The tenth day is likely to be fatal; those who fall sick will rarely recover, but the 2bild born on this day will live long and be a great traveler.

11.   The child that is born on the eleventh day will be much devoted to religion and have an engaging form and manners.

12. On the twelfth day the dreams are rather fortunate, and the child burn shall live long.

13. On the thirteenth day the dreams will prove true in a very short time.

14. If you ask a favor of any one on the fourteenth day, it will be granted.

15. The sickness that befalls a person on the fifteenth day is likely to prove mortal.

16. The child that is born on the sixteenth day will be of very ill-manners and unfortunate; it is nevertheless a good day for the buying and selling of all kinds of merchandise.

17. The child born on the seventeenth day will be very foolish; it is a very unfortunate day to transact any kind of business, or contract marriage.

18. The child born on the eighteenth day will be vigilant, but will suffer considerable hardships; if a female, she will be chaste and industrious, and live respected to n great age.

19. The nineteenth day is dangerous; the child born will be very ill-disposed and malicious.

20. On the twentieth day the dreams are true, but the child born will be dishonest.

21. The child born on the twenty-first day will grow up healthy and strong, but be of a very selfish, ungenteel turn of mind.

22. The child born on the twenty-second day will be fortunate; he or she will be of a cheerful countenance, religious, and much be loved.

23. The child that is born on the twenty-third day will be of an ungovernable temper, will forsake his friends, and choose to wander about in a foreign country, and will be very unhappy through life.

24. The child born on the twenty-fourth day will achieve many heroic actions, and will be much admired for his extraordinary abilities.

25. The child born on the twenty-fifth day will be very wicked; he will meet with many dangers, and is likely to come to an ill end.

26. On the twenty-sixth day the dreams are certain - the child then born will be rich, and much esteemed.

27. The twenty-seventh day is very favorable for dreams, and the child then born will be of a sweet and humble disposition.

28. The child born the twenty-eighth day will be the delight of his parents, but will not live to any great age.

29. Children born on the twenty-ninth day will experience many hardships, though in the end they may turn out happily. It is good to marry on this day; and business begun on this day will be prosperous.

30. The child that is born on the thirtieth day will be fortunate and happy, and well skilled in the arts and sciences.

TO CAST YOUR NATIVITY

Having ascertained the exact time of your birth, and the hour in which you entered this transitory life, procure a Moore's almanac of that year, which will direct you to the sign that then reigned, the name of the planets, and the state of the moon; particularly observe whether the sun was just entering the sign, whether it was near the end, or what was its particular progress; if at the beginning, your fate will be strongly tinctured with its properties, moderate at the meridian, and slightly if the sun is nearly going out of the Write down the day of the week; see whether it is a lucky day or not, the state of the moon, the nature of the planets, and the influence described next, and you will ascertain your future destiny with very little trouble.

The Sealed Magical Book of Moses

JANUARY
(Aquarius or the Water Bearer.)
Gives a love of wandering and variety, seldom contented long in one place; soon affronted, and slow to forgive; fond of law, though they lose the day. They are unhappy. Mercury gives them slights in love. A full moon is the best, for a new moon only adds to their false fears; and Saturn gives them real trouble to content with.

FEBRUARY
(Pisces, or the Fishes.)
Those born under the influence of this planet prosper beat on the ocean, or at a distance from their native home. But those born under this sign, and not ordained to travel, will experience at times more or less distress. Mars and Jupiter are the best planets, and if the day of the week on which they, were born be a fortunate one, let them begin their fresh concerns on that day, write and answer letters, or seek for money due to them according to their rule, and they have more than a chance for prosperity. The female traveler will be very fortunate, and have a contempt for danger, yet neither her disposition nor manners will be masculine; she will make an excellent wife and mother, and, if left a widow with children, will strive for their interest with a father's care and prudence; nor will she wed a second time, unless Venus rules her destiny, liars give her success; Jupiter, vigilance; a new moon, virtue; a full moon, some enemies; and Saturn, temptation; yet she will prosper.

MARCH
(Aries, or the Ram.)
A very good sign to those born under it To either sex denotes prosperity, fidelity, dutiful children, and many liberal friends, but hot-tempered; if Mercury Is one of the planets, they will then be very amiable. Jupiter and Venus are also good planets to them, but Mars or Saturn causes a sad alteration to their general destiny, and gives a mixed life of wine and pleasure. Venus reigning alone as a morning star at the time of their birth causes them many amours.

APRIL
(Taurus, or the Bull.)
To be prosperous under this sign will require active industry and patience under misfortunes and perils; but Jupiter, Venus, or the new moon, will soften this destiny. The men will be bold and adventurous, fond of governing, and hard to please; they must be careful not to enter on any fresh concern while their sign has the ascendancy, the end of April and the tw6 first weeks in May.

The Sealed Magical Book of Moses

MAY
(Gemini, or the Twins) Very fortunate for females, particularly in the grand article of matrimony, though they will prosper well in other affairs; the full moon and Venus are good for them. They will be punctual and honest in their dealings, be much respected by their friends and neighbors, and have many children.

JUNE
(Cancer, or the Crab)
A prosperous but eventful sign to both sexes, but more particularly those of a fair complexion; they will be exalted in life; Jupiter and Venus are the best signs for them; but the brunettes, though fortunate, will plague themselves and others with whims, curiosities, and ill-nature, and may be particular about mere trifles. If Man be their planet, they will enter into lawsuits; and if Saturn; let them beware of ungovernable passions.

JULY
(Leo, or the Lion)
Favorable to those born in poverty, but not to the rich; for this sign always shows a great change of circumstances about the meridian of our days, sooner or later, according to the sign in which you were born. If Jupiter be the planet, the person born poor will become rich by legacies, or will probably marry their master or mistress, or his or her son or daughter, according to their sex, and lead a happy life. This has often proved true.

AUGUST
(Virgo, or the Virgin)
A most important sign; the men brave, generous, candid, and honest; the females amicable and prosperous, If they do not mar their own fortune by love of flattery, to which they will be prone, or else advancement awaits them. Venus is not a good planet for them, and Saturn shows seduction; but, if neither of these three planets predominate at the time of their birth, they will marry early, have good children, and enjoy the most valuable blessings of life, and have many unexpected gains.

SEPTEMBER
(Libra, or the Balance)
A middle course of life is promised by this sign; a smooth, even, unrippled stream, free from storms or sudden changes; in fact, an enviable destiny. The persons now born will be just in their transactions, faithful in love and wedlock, and averse to litigation and law; not many children, but those healthy.

OCTOBER
(Scorpio, or the Scorpion)
To the man, promises a long, active, useful life, and an intelligent mind; prosperous and very careful of what he gains; a good husband, parent and master, and a sincere friend; a little gay in his youthful days, but not vicious. Jupiter and a full moon add to the good of his destiny; Saturn or Mercury will detract from it; Venus inclines him to the fair sex. To the woman this sign shows indolence; and, if she is well off in the world, it will not be by her own merit or industry, for she will have to thank those to whom it is her good fortune to be nearly allied; but, If she has no shining qualities that are prominent, she will be free from evil propensies, and will never bring disgrace on herself, her husband, her family, or friends, unless Venus reigned at her birth; then I fear for her; but no other planet will affect her destiny.

NOVEMBER
(Sagittarius, or the Archer)
Gives to both sexes an amorous disposition, and if Venus or Mercury presides at their birth, they will love variety; out Jupiter and Mars are good for them; the new moon is excellent to the female, add full to the man. It is seldom that persons born in this sign marry, if the first-mentioned planets reign; or, if they do marry, it is late in life, or when the meridian of their days are over, and they are become wise enough to relinquish folly; they then become steady and prudent, and generally do well; they seldom have many children, but what they have will prosper, and have friends who will promote their interest.

DECEMBER
(Capricorn, or the Goat)
Shows you will work and toil, and others reap the benefit of your labor, unless marriage) alters the destiny; out hard will be your fate if your spouse is of the same sign as yourself; but. If Jupiter be one of the planets at your birth, the end of your days will be more prosperous than the beginning, after experiencing many cares and obstructions. A woman may probably better her fate by a second marriage, especially if Venus be her planet.

LOVE PRESENTS AND WITCHING SPELLS

Take three hairs from your head, roll them up in a small compact form, and anoint them with three drops of blood from the left-hand fourth finger, choosing tills because the anatomists say a vein goes from that finger to the heart; wear this In your bosom (taking care that none knows the secret) for nine days and nights; then enclose the hair in the secret cavity of a ring or a brooch, and present it to your lover. While it is in his possession, it will have the effect of preserving his love, and leading his mind to dwell on you.

A chain or plait of your own hair, mixed with that of a goat, and anointed with nine drops of the essence of ambergris, will have a similar effect.

Flowers prepared with your own blood will have an effect on your lover's mind; but the impression will be very transient, and fade with the flowers. If your love should be fortunate, and you are married to the object of your wishes, never reveal to him the nature of the present you made him, or it may have the fatal effect of turning love into hate.

HOLY INCANTATIONS FROM THE BIBLE

CURE FOR THE COLIC

Take one fresh chicken egg and turn the small end three times in the navel of the sick baby. Say this Bible verse out loud over the baby:

Behold, if a river overflow, he trembleth not; He is confident, though a Jordan swell even to his mouth.
Job 40:23

Then bury the egg on the North end of the house.

The mother of the baby should then burn a white onion in hog lard and remove the burnt pieces. Mash this up to make a salve and rub this on the baby's stomach morning and night for nine days. On the ninth day the baby will stop crying.

STOP PAIN

Find a smooth creek stone big enough to fit into the palm of your hand. Hold the stone on the forehead of the one who is in pain and say the following chant:

Hair and hide,
Flesh and blood,
Nerve and bone,
No more pain than this stone.

Next say the following Bible verse:

and they lifted up their voices, saying,
Jesus, Master, have mercy on us.
Luke 17:13

TO LIFT A CURSE

If someone complains of being cursed, lay your hands on their shoulders and silently say the following:

Lord Jesus, thy wounds so red will guard me against death. Lord Jesus, thy suffering so profound will guard me against pain. Lord Jesus, thy tears so cleansing will guard me against evil.

TO RELEASE SOMEONE WHO IS SPELL-BOUND

This can be done for someone who is in your presence or at a distance. If the person is far-away, make sure no creek or river is between you. Say this out loud:

You horseman and footman, whom I here conjured at this time, you may pass on in the name of Jesus Christ, through the word of God and the will of Christ; ride ye on now and pass.

Next, read this Bible verse to yourself:

Unto the upright there ariseth light in the darkness: He is' gracious, and merciful, and righteous.
Psalms 112:4

TO BE BLESSED AT ALL TIMES

To be assured of Gods blessing everyday, say this silently to yourself in the morning upon arising from bed:

I conjure thee, sword, sabre or knife, that mightest injure or harm me, by the priest of all prayers, who had gone into the temple at Jerusalem, and said: An edged sword shall pierce your soul that you may not injure me, who am a child of God.

The Sealed Magical Book of Moses

TO ASSURE GOD'S BLESSING TO A LOVED ONE

If there is someone you love and want them to receive God's blessing and protection, without telling them what you are doing, say their name out loud when the sun rises in the morning and then say silently:

Like unto the cup and the wine, and the holy supper, which our dear Lord Jesus Christ gave unto his dear disciples on Maunday Thursday, may the Lord Jesus guard [name] in daytime, and at night, that no dog may bite [name], no wild beast tear [name] to pieces, no tree fall on [name], no water rise against [name], no fire-arms injure [name], no weapons, no steel, no iron, cut [name], no fire burn [name], no false sentence fall upon [name], no false tongue injure [name], no rogue enrage [name], and that no fiends, no witchcraft and enchantment can harm [name]. Amen.

TO SPELL-BIND ANYTHING

Say the Lord's Prayer three times, then say:

Christ's cross and Christ's crown, Christ Jesus' colored blood, be thou every hour good. God, the Father, is before me; God, the Son, is beside me; God, the Holy Ghost, is behind me. Whoever now is stronger than these three persons may come, by day or night, to attack me.

A CURE FOR WOUNDS

Take the bones of a calf, and burn them until they turn to powder, and then strew it into the wound. Next, recite this Bible verse:

Receive him therefore in the Lord with all joy; and hold such in honor: because for the work of Christ he came nigh unto death, hazarding his life to supply that which was lacking in your service toward me.
Philippians 2:29-30

The powder prevents the flesh from putrefying, and is therefore of great importance in healing the wound. Another cure is for cuts and scratches on a child. Place both of your hands on the head of a hurt child and say:

Mother Mary stop thy crying, Mother Mary stop thy pain. With your son's blood speak truth from these lips.

The Sealed Magical Book of Moses

A REMEDY FOR BURNS

To relieve the pain and heal a burn, say this Bible verse to yourself:
Now the God of hope fill you with all joy and peace in believing, that ye may abound in hope, in the power of the Holy Spirit. Romans 15:13

Next, say this out loud:

Clear out, brand, but never in; be thou cold or hot, thou must cease to burn. May God guard thy blood and thy flesh, thy marrow and thy bones, and every artery, great or small. They all shall be guarded and protected in the name of God against inflammation and mortification, in the name of God the Father, the Son, and the Holy Ghost. Amen.

This can be done in the presence of those that are injured, or to heal someone from a distance.

A WAY TO FIND LOVE FOR THOSE WHO SEEK

Take a piece of red ribbon and wrap it three times around the wrist of those seeking love. With each wrap, say these words:

Oh Song of Songs find thee love. Oh Song of Songs bring thee love. Oh Song of Songs keep thee love.

Wear the ribbon for three days and at the end of the third day, remove the ribbon and place it in a Bible to insure God's blessing.

KEEP POVERTY AT BAY

To keep poverty from taking everything away from you or a friend, take a length of black thread from an unused spool. Starting from the bottom, tie seven knots throughout the length of the thread and recite out loud with each knot:

For we are God's workmanship, created in Christ Jesus to do good works, which God prepared in advance for us to do. Ephesians 2:10

Place the thread in a small bag and whoever needs it, carry it with him at all times to keep poverty away.

The Sealed Magical Book of Moses

FOR A DIFFICULT PREGNANCY

If a woman is worried that the baby she is carrying will be premature or breach, take a bowl of fresh rainwater and dip your finger in it. With your wet finger, make the sign of the cross on the stomach of the pregnant woman and say out loud:

May it please thee O, Eel Chad, to grant unto this woman [name] daughter of [name], that she may not at this time, or at any other time, have a premature confinement; much more grant unto her a truly fortunate delivery, and keep her and the fruit of the body in good health.

If a woman is having trouble conceiving, say this:

Lord and Lady. Mother and Father. Life Divine. Gift [name] with a healthy child.

TO HAVE GOOD FORTUNE

This is for anyone who has been unlucky despite their best efforts. Say this Bible verse three times before the sun rises:

And they that are wise shall shine as the brightness of the firmament; and they that turn many to righteousness as the stars for ever and ever.
Daniel 12:3

TO OVERCOME WICKED PEOPLE

To stop anyone who means to do you or your loved ones harm, say the following Bible verse:

One of themselves, a prophet of their own, said, Cretans are always liars, evil beasts, idle gluttons.
Titus 1:12

PROTECT YOUR HOME AND BELONGINGS

Write the following sacred names on a clean piece of white paper:

SATOR, AREPO, TENET, OPERA, ROTAS.

Seal them in a small bag that can be tied or sewn shut. Place the bag near your front door.

CURE FOR THE HEADACHE

Tame thou flesh and bone, like Christ in Paradise; and who will assist thee, this I tell thee [name] for your repentance sake.

This you must say three times, each time lasting for three minutes, and your headache will soon cease.

TO LIVE HAPPY AND BE PROSPEROUS

Say this verse once a day, every day:

Thou wilt shew me the path of life; in thy presence is fullness of joy; at thy right hand there are pleasures for evermore.
Psalms 16:11

DREAMS

How to Receive Oracles by Dreams

He who would receive true dreams, should keep a pure, undisturbed, and imaginative spirit, and so compose it that it may be made worthy of knowledge and government by the mind; for such a spirit is most fit for prophesying, and is a most clear glass of all images which flow everywhere from all things. When, therefore, we are sound in body, not disturbed in mind, our intellect not made dull by heavy meats and strong drink, not sad through poverty, not provoked through lust, not incited by any vice, nor stirred up by wrath or anger, not being irreligiously and profanely inclined, not given to levity nor lost to drunkenness, but, chastely going to bed, fall asleep, then our pure and divine soul being free from all the evils above recited, and separated from all hurtful thoughts-and now freed, by dreaming is endowed with this divine spirit as an instrument, and doth receive those beams and representations which are darted down, as it were, and shine forth from, the divine Hind into itself, in a deifying glass.

The Sealed Magical Book of Moses

There are four kinds of true dreams, viz., the first, matutine, i.e., between sleeping and waking; the second, that which one sees concerning another; the third, that whose interpretation is shown to the same dreamer in the nocturnal vision; and, lastly, that which-is related to the same dreamer in the nocturnal vision. But natural things and their own co-mixtures do likewise belong unto wise men, and we often use such to receive oracles from a spirit by a dream, which are either by perfumes, unctions, meats, drinks, rings, seals, etc.

Now those who are desirous to receive oracles through a dream, let them make themselves a ring of the Sun or Saturn for this purpose. There are likewise images of dreams, which, being put under the head when going to sleep, doth effectually give true dreams of whatever the mind hath before determined or consulted upon, the practice of which is as follows:

Thou Shalt make an image of the Sun, the figure whereof must be a man sleeping upon the bosom of an angel; which thou shall make when Leo ascends, the Sun being in the ninth house in Aries; then you must write upon the figure the name of the effect desired, and in the hand of the angel the name and character of the intelligence of the Sun, which is Michael.

Let the same Image be made in Virgo ascending--Mercury being fortunate in Aries in the ninth, or Gemini ascending, Mercury being fortunate in the ninth house in Aquarius and let him be received by Saturn with a fortunate aspect, and let the name of the spirit (which is Raphael) be written upon it. Let the same likewise be made-Libra ascending, Venus being received from Mercury in Gemini in the ninth house-and write upon it the name of the angel of Venus (which is Anacl). Again you may make the same image-Aquarius ascending, Saturn fortunately possessing the ninth in his exaltation, which is Libra-and let there be written upon it the name of the angel of Saturn (which is Cassial). The same may be made with Cancer ascending, the Moon being received by Jupiter and Venus in Pisces, and being fortunately placed in the ninth house-and write upon it the spirit of the Moon (which is Gabriel).

There are likewise made rings of dreams of wonderful efficacy, and there are rings of the Sun and Saturn-and the constellation of them in, when the Sun or Saturn ascend in their exaltation in the ninth, and when the Moon is joined to Saturn in the ninth, and in that sign which was the ninth house of the nativity, and write and engrave upon the rings the name of the spirit of the Sun or Saturn; and by these rules you may know how and by what means to constitute more of yourself.

But know this, that such images work nothing (as they are simply images), except they are vivified by spiritual and celestial virtue, and chiefly by the ardent desire and firm intent of the soul of the operator. But who can give a soul to an image, or make a stone, or metal, or clay, or wood, or wax, or paper, to live? Certainly no man whatever; for this arcanum doth not enter into an artist of a stiff neck. He only hath it who transcends the progress of angels, and comes to the very Archtype Himself. The tables of numbers likewise confer to the receiving of oracles, being duly formed under their own constellations.

Therefore, he who is desirous of receiving true oracles by dreams, let him abstain from supper, from drink, and be otherwise well disposed, so his brain will be free from turbulent vapors; let him also have his bed-chamber fair and clean, exorcised and consecrated; then let him perfume the same with some convenient fumigation, and let him anoint his temples with some unguent efficacious hereunto, and put a ring of dreams upon his finger; then let him take one of the images we have spoken of, and place the same under his head; then let him address himself to sleep, meditating upon that thing which he desires to know. So shall he receive a most certain and undoubted oracle by a dream when the Moon goes through the sign of the ninth revolution of his nativity, and when she is in the ninth sign from the sign of perfection.

This is the way whereby we may obtain all sciences and arts whatsoever, whether astrology, occult philosophy, physic, etc. or else suddenly and perfectly with a true Illumination of our Intellect, although all inferior familiar spirits whatsoever conduce to this effect, and sometimes also evil spirits sensibly inform us, intrinsically and extrinsically.

FINGER-NAIL OBSERVATIONS

Broad nails show the person to be bashful, fearful, but of gentle nature.

When there is a certain white mark at the extremity of them, it shows that the person has more honesty than subtlety, and that his worldly substance will be impaired through negligence.

Long white nails denote much sickness and infirmity, especially fevers, an indication of strength and deceit by women. If upon the white anything appears at the extremity that is pale, it denotes short life by sudden death, and the person to be given to melancholy.

The Sealed Magical Book of Moses

When there appears a certain mixed redness, of colors, at the beginning of the nails, it shows the person to be choleric and quarrelsome.

When the extremity is black it is a sign of husbandry.

Narrow nails denote the person to be inclined to mischief and to do injury to his neighbor.

Long nails show the person to be good-natured, but mistrustful, and loves reconciliation rather than differences.

Oblique nails signify deceit and want of courage, little and round nails denote obstinate anger and hatred. If they be crooked at the extremity, they show pride and fierceness.

Round nails show a choleric person, yet soon reconciled, honest, and a lover of secret sciences.

Fleshy nails denote the person to be mild in his temper, idle, and lazy pale and black nails show the person to he very deceitful to his neighbor, and subject to many diseases.

Red and marked nails signify a choleric and martial nature, given to cruelty; and, as many little marks aft there are, they speak of so many evil desires.

TRADITIONAL WAY TO BAFFLE YOUR ENEMIES

Repeat reverently, and with sincere faith, the following words, and you will be protected in the hour of danger:

"Behold, God is my salvation; I will trust, and not be afraid, for the Lord Jehovah is my strength and my song; he also is become my salvation.
"For the stars of heaven, and the constellation thereof, shall not give their light; the sun shall be darkened in his going forth, and the moon shall not cause her tight to shine.

"And behold, at eventide, trouble; and before morning he is not; this is the portion of them that spoil us, and the lot of them that rob us."

CHARM AGAINST TROUBLE IN GENERAL

Repeat reverently, and with sincere faith, the following words, and you shall be protected in the hour of danger:

"He shall deliver thee in six troubles, yea, in seven there shall no evil touch thee; in famine he shall redeem thee from death, and in war from the power of the sword; and thou shall know that thy tabernacle shall be in peace, and thou shalt visit thy habitation and shall not err."

Write for our free catalog:

Global Communications
P.O. Box 753
New Brunswick, NJ 08903

www.conspiracyjournal.com

Made in the USA
Las Vegas, NV
29 March 2024